GOLDEN RULE MANAGEMENT

To Ken,
A friend though
thick and thin!
Best wishes for
great success!

5-3-94

STEPHEN J. HOLOVIAK

GOLDEN RULE MANAGEMENT

GIVE RESPECT, GET RESULTS

Every person is a valued asset. Have fun with the Golden Rule.

Sincerely,

ADDISON-WESLEY PUBLISHING COMPANY, INC.

Reading, Massachusetts • Menlo Park, California • New York
Don Mills, Ontario • Wokingham, England • Amsterdam
Bonn • Paris • Milan • Madrid • Sidney • Singapore
Tokyo • Seoul • Taipei • Mexico City • San Juan

The publisher offers discounts on this book when ordered in quantity for special sales. For more information please contact:

Corporate & Professional Publishing Group
Addison-Wesley Publishing Company
One Jacob Way
Reading, Massachusetts 01867

Library of Congress Cataloging-in-Publication Data

Holoviak, Stephen J.
Golden rule management : give respect, get results / Stephen J. Holoviak.
p. cm.
Includes bibliographical references and index.
ISBN 0-201-63333-7
1. Management. 2. Communication in management. 3. Golden rule. I. Title.
HD31.H617 1993
658–dc20
92-41300
CIP

Cover design by Hannus Design Associates
Text design by Wilson Graphics & Design (Kenneth J. Wilson)
Set in 10 point Palatino by Camden Type 'n Graphics

ISBN 0-201-63333-7

Text printed on recycled and acid-free paper.
1 2 3 4 5 6 7 8 9 10 MA 96959493
First Printing: May 1993

Contents

Acknowledgments

The process of Golden Rule Management began long ago, and over the years many brave and farsighted friends have allowed me to try unconventional ideas in their respective organizations. I can never include everyone or thank each of them sufficiently.

The decision about where to begin to thank people for their help, trust, and support is a hard one. Do I go back to my major doctoral adviser Dr. Fred Zeller and his hours of discussion with me about organization efficiency? Do I go further back and actually thank the first boss who "mismanaged" me and started the process rolling? Mike Murry who was with Rohr Industries at its Hagerstown, Maryland, plant shared with me many creative ideas being implemented at that facility. Mike's ideas kept me motivated about the operational prospects of this type of managerial style.

I know there have been many who have had faith—a great deal of faith to allow me to try what in many cases were new and untried ideas. Tom and Gretchen Carbaugh believed in the concept enough to allow revolutionary ideas to be used in a subsidiary of American Visions Corporation. It was a leap of faith for them. My thanks to Dr. Robert Ackelsberg for his help on projects and many discussions and sharing of experiences.

The backing of Marcella Davidson and Cedric Long of the H. B. Reese Candy Company, who displayed the ideal form and backing of senior manager support, is much appreciated. Cedric Long, the manager of Employee Relations at Reese at the time, and I spent many hours putting our heads together to come up with new approaches and ideas. In like form, Joe Maher of Hershey Chocolate Company was a strong supporter of the new concepts and ideas. Joe participated in the process and offered constructive criticism. Many other people at Reese and Hershey also provided guidance, help, and support during the past twelve years.

At JLG Industries, my appreciation goes out to Sam Swope, senior vice president of Human Resource Management, and Dave Black, president, both strong supporters of the program. At the San Georgio Pasta plant, Thomas DeAngelis, plant manager, showed great courage in supporting Task Team Bargaining. Others who went out on a limb there included

Dr. David DeCenzo and Sharon Holoviak, cofacilitators; Earl Light from the Bakery, Confectionery and Tobacco Workers Union Local 464; Shirley Gable, chief plant steward; and Jack Minnich of MANTEC, the industrial resource center of Southcentral Pennsylvania. All played a role in the creation of Task Team Bargaining in the Golden Rule environment.

Bob Zullinger, president of Farmers and Merchants Trust Company, and the staff shared ideas and allowed us to present our mission of how supervisors could be handled in financial/service organizations. Thanks also to Steve Wagner, my friend at Federal Express, for some early ideas and guidance.

Others who have offered counsel include Martin B. Skane, manager of Human Resources, Teledyne Landis Machine; Americ Azevedo, president of Octagon Corporation; Judith Roales, president/publisher, Delaware State News; former dean Joseph Hunt, College of Business, Shippensburg University; W. E. Matthews, Sr., Corning Glassworks; and Dr. Robert Figler, University of Akron. I thank my close friend and philosopher, Tom Bowen, who has challenged me with new ideas and viewpoints and contributed new concepts of human belief for me to test.

Of course, the typist Joyce Yocum, who exhibited considerable patience with my rewrites and changes of direction, deserves a strong note of appreciation.

A number of people both officially and unofficially reviewed this work: Tom Webb, Dave Showalter, Bob Figler, and Dave DeCenzo to name a few. I think their ideas added to the quality. My appreciation is extended to Jerry Sanders of Alloy Rods, Hanover, Pennsylvania, and Darlene Caplan of GTE, York, Pennsylvania, for their review and encouragement. My connections with various organizations have offered opportunities to learn from committee work and peer associations. My tenure on the education committee of the Association for Quality and Participation (AQP) was significant in providing new thoughts and contacts. In similar form, my involvement with the Advanced Employee Involvement Practitioners Lab held in Linden Hall, Pennsylvania, has been of great value.

Finally, my wife Sharon, who I respect for her knowledge of people, added considerably to the success of the program. Thanks also to my children, Stephen, Kelly, and Justin, who share their views on people, and Brooke, from whom I have learned much about respect and dignity.

Chapter 1

BUILDING BRIDGES

The following pages introduce a philosophy of life for management, an approach to dealing with people that is simple yet very effective. In fact, its simplicity is the reason for its effectiveness. The root concept is dignity and respect for people, treating workers as valued assets and always as adults. If you are confused about which action to take with people, always take the action that results in trust, respect, and a higher self-image—the way *you* would like to be treated.

> If you are confused about which action to take with people, always take the action that results in trust, respect, and a higher self-image—the way *you* would like to be treated.

In the chapters that follow, you will see how Golden Rule Management works operationally in our performance appraisal systems, our career paths, and our training programs. The outcome is committed workers producing more products and services of higher quality. Plus, you will be acting as a facilitator of people's growth, not being the "bad guy" or "fire fighter" or someone's "mom" or "dad." Both the employee and the supervisor gain from the Golden Rule concept.

The Golden Rule concept deals with letting go: letting go of unnecessary work rules, letting go of the need to feel powerful in our positions. It means changing our current managerial beliefs about our positions. The need for power and control in so many areas creates a lot of our problems. Let's shed that yoke and move forward.

Most people want themselves to be considered a "total person" or a "real person." This is how we would like to be treated. Let's use this feeling of authenticity with our workers as a foundation on which to build a work relationship, a foundation for solid communication. It is a simple concept, but in many aspects of life we look for complex solutions when the obvious solution is right there in front of us. Football is basically block, tackle, and

1

run. Vince Lombardi always stressed these basic, simple concepts, and the results were dramatic.

ACCEPTING EMOTIONS

This book is also going to deal with emotion. Yes, emotion. For many years, American management looked on "emotion" as an ugly word, a word that had no place in the cold, hard realities of the business world. Our nonwork world was suppose to be used for the more emotional aspects of handling our lives. This book, however, deals a lot with emotion. This book is about feelings. It is about the fact that people possess emotions and feelings and cannot be treated as if they are a piece of machinery, void of such feelings. Perhaps the concept of emotionally void decision-making began with our scientific method, in which things had to be based on hard facts. I don't know. But our idea of the rational man, a logical thinking being, permeated many aspects of our life in business. This rather straightforward, machine-like thinking has tended to reduce our inner and deeper actions with individual workers and relegate them to a lower platform, somewhere lower in value to that of a piece of machinery. The beauty of the Golden Rule approach is that control over one's own destiny is returned. We can move with a renewed sense of self-respect as we accept back this control over our lives.

When we spoke in the past about handling people properly, some rather straightforward techniques were used to deal with the facts of the problem. We figured that with logical deduction and scientific reasoning we could reach an appropriate solution. It hasn't been that many years ago that I remember going to work and having my boss tell me, "Stephen, you have to leave your personal problems at home. You have to be professional on the job, you can't get emotional about these things." My boss had no idea what was on my mind, what the topic of my problem was, or anything else. He just saw that there was an emotional response in me, and he didn't think it was professional and felt it should be put away. This early supervisor was not the exception. Various management writers over the years have echoed a similar theme:

> As contextual thinkers, managers are sparing in their relationships. They make few attachments, and above all, they keep their emotions to themselves. Emotional attachments create obligations or a feeling of entitlement that managers are not prepared to accept. Once managers feel that other individuals have a legitimate claim on them for a benefit or reward, the managers' freedom of action is limited by the weight of guilt. Managers, therefore, are willing to accept people for the role they play, but not for the expectations beyond the confines of the role. (Zaleznik, 1989)

The process discussed in this book takes an entirely different tactic, a tactic that has been tried by this author and others successfully over a long period. We are going to build bridges with employees. We are going to stress building emotional bridges. From a very basic motivational standpoint, the more bridges we build, the more potential avenues there are to gain employee commitment. The goal is to solve a problem, not to put it away. This sends the message that we are going to deal with employees as total persons. We are not just dealing with them as a slice of the issue. It lets employees know that we understand the emotional base from which they are coming and will deal with the total problem and all aspects of the situation.

We must stress building emotional bridges with people.

CHOOSING A DIFFERENT PATH

Now that we have discussed the "why" of Golden Rule Management, let's discuss how. I have authored previous books and a number of articles and have tried to explain bits and pieces of the Golden Rule concept. Unfortunately, it has never been called the Golden Rule Management concept. For the most part, the books and articles are technical, and a lot of people haven't read them. Of those who have, many didn't understand them. In fact, many times readers asked, "Why don't you just say this in plain English?" Well, this book attempts to do just that. Traditional writing for academics and consultants is rather matter of fact. It is scientific in nature. Most of my books have been research based, and many of my articles are research based. They take on the third-person, detached component of a scientific observer, carefully and dispassionately analyzing the data. Well, I have tried that and it failed. This isn't dispassionate, this comes from my heart, and it is in plain English.

I have written a number of articles dealing with career paths, training, communications systems, and participative management. Many of these articles track data over a time frame of years. The results are striking and they almost speak for themselves. The articles received positive recognition from the scientific community and the academic community. Some even called the research talented and revealing. The problem was that the only people reading the literature were other scientists and researchers and people like myself. The message wasn't getting through in a strong enough fashion to the people who could benefit from it, and that was the business people—the managers on the assembly line. It missed the worker for the state government who has to supervise a number of people who are not paid well or are not on an incentive system. It is for managers who have no way of rewarding any of their workers if they do the task correctly. This book is written for all the people working in foreign-owned corporations who may not have the vaguest idea of who is the parent company. It is written for those who may never see their bosses because they are thousands of miles away and, therefore, feel that their bosses don't really care. There are many "bosses" who just want an investment in a stable economy with a stable currency, and the United States fits the bill. These are the people in everyday life who have real emotions and real problems and want to know how to get results. They need to get results or they will end up getting fired.

I listened to the famous writer and consultant, Tom Peters, speak. I thought the most exciting quality of this dynamic man was that he spoke from the heart. He wrote from the heart, and I thought, there is a message for me. Outside the field of management, I have read the works of other writers who seemed to be getting through to some of the people and I suspect they were writing from the heart, that they were addressing the issue directly to the people.

I have a different set of problems than Tom Peters. I'm not trying to get through to the chairman of the board, or the president, because I think Tom Peters and some other writers like him do that very well. I'm trying to get through to middle management and the first-line supervisors. I truly believe the turnaround in America is going to come from the success of our first-line supervisors. The true market, the true readers for this work are the middle and first-line managers, the ones on whom the turnaround will eventually rest. In this book the scientific jargon, complex statistics, regression analyses, and similar tools are left behind. I would like to talk about things I have tried in plain English. The Golden Rule concept is simple and easy to use. It is something we can identify with in the middle of the first-line supervisory ranks. Will top managers ever read this book? The benefits to them of reading it would be significant. If they read this book, they can help their first-line supervisors succeed by understanding what they need to be doing in order to return quality, excellence, and dignity to the workplace.

Company names will be used in sharing examples, but they are not being held up for view as the role model or the mold for change. They are examples of specific situations at a point in time that worked. Why this avoidance of role models? Just look to the examples used in Tom Peters's first book; almost to the case they have regressed since the book's publication. We are not trying to say, look at these companies and follow their path. We are not trying to produce clones from this book. The goal is to change your mind and your managerial life-style and to develop your own frame of reference and philosophy. Most important, when we change to fit a role model we then try to hold the status quo. There can be no "running in place" in organizations. Change is the constant we can count on for the future.

> There can be no "running in place" in organizations. Change is the constant we can count on for the future.

The achievement of dignity and respect—the Golden Rule—in our workplaces is an ongoing process, a kind of spiritual climb toward perfection. This means we will be ever changing in the journey toward this goal. I believe it is this realization that will keep the Golden Rule concept from stagnation and decline.

Chapter 2

ROOTS OF THE IDEA

As we review the program of Golden Rule Management, it will appear to contain roots of various origins. Yet, it is packaged in a fluid and easy-to-handle arrangement. It is an arrangement of ideas gathered over decades of research, and decades of being an employee, an employee subject to many types of managerial styles.

Being particularly observant by nature, I cataloged the various experiences in my life—what I liked, my feelings, my joys and motivations, and how these affected the product or service I was hired to produce or perform. Over the years I've kept, and still keep today, a diary of these operational ideas, feelings, and emotions about job-related issues. This diary has served me well. For example, in my first weeks on the job as a new operations manager trainee for Merrill Lynch, I recorded everything that didn't make sense to me, things that were illogical and inefficient. When I was promoted, this diary became my reference book, and I began using these comments as a basis for implementing changes. The first office where I was in charge of operations was ranked at the bottom within its region in terms of efficiency. The changes helped move it up significantly. The next steps were the first attempts at forming the Golden Rule Management process, which eventually boosted my office to the position of top-rated efficiency office in the region.

At Merrill Lynch, training reflected the current managerial philosophies of the time. The "managed" people were skilled workers in a fast-paced, service-oriented area. The whole system was geared toward individual achievement. The effect of people working only for their own job areas could easily be seen as inefficient. The sales staff was perceived as higher in status than the operations staff and often interacted only under duress from management. The reality was that both sides needed each other to deliver top-quality service to the client. When a stockbroker and sales assistant took the time to team up with a good operations clerk and others in the "back office," the results were superb. They worked for the common good of the client and all the office employees felt a sense of pride in the success of the stockbroker. On the other extreme was the stockbroker who never fostered this relationship and regularly complained to me (as operations manager) that he got "lousy" service and the operations people didn't care about his clients. Yet, these same operations people were bending over backward for the other broker who used the Golden Rule approach and achieved superb results.

The influence of the top manager on the staff was obvious. When an office manager followed an autocratic system, there was little I could do as operations manager to raise efficiency levels. The autocratic system suppressed creative thinking and problem solving and lowered self-esteem. This, of course, costs dearly in terms of individual commitment. Many of us worked hard during this time in our careers, often fifty to sixty hours a week. Implementing many of the recorded items from my diary raised the efficiency ranking, yet it was not enough. Then the top management of the office changed to a more participative style of leadership. This allowed me to use my first ideas about Golden Rule Management. As mentioned, the success created by it boosted our office ranking to the top in the region. Opportunities for decentralized authority were first put into effect. Authority was decentralized by moving both the responsibility and authority for a job as close to the operating level as possible. For example, a receiving clerk would decide if stock was a "good delivery" with all the necessary papers. The operations manager was not required to approve every receipt of stock. Next, we formed a few autonomous work teams. The "wire room" where orders were sent and the "cage" where securities were handled were natural places for workgroups without traditional supervision. These work teams were part of the process to set standards for the job and determine when a job was well done. Traditional supervision was only necessary when there were deviations from the standard or highly exceptional circumstances. The reality became that people were trusted as adults, the way I would have wanted to be treated. Plus, they were very competent in their jobs. The fit was perfect.

Was this my first encounter with observing management styles? No. This pilgrimage began years before and covered numerous jobs along the way. But it was the first time where I was in a position to implement some changes. Some earlier encounters included the following:

- My days as a theater usher influenced my reactions as a low-paid service worker. Basically, ushers are "nonpersons" who are overlooked by the consuming public. If not handled correctly, the employees in these environments may be disruptive or indifferent to the client. This may harm the establishment in terms of a lost client. It taught me the difficulty of gaining commitment from low-paid service workers and how critical it is to gain trust.

- Working both the 3 P.M. to 11 P.M. and 11 P.M. to 7 A.M. shifts in a food processing plant resulted in numerous entries in the diary of ideas. It was my first encounter with the "good-old-boy" system of promoting friends. I learned about work "pranks" such as how to jam a machine or derail a conveyor to get a break. I found out firsthand how boring an assembly line can get if people are not emotionally part of the process. I watched industrial engineers and accountants plan changes to work areas without ever asking advice. We all hoped their changes would work; many times they did not. Those of us on the line could have helped. I never knew how my job related to anything else in the plant, its mission, or goals. For that matter most of us were not even sure what the rest of the operation looked like, or how much it cost to make the product. There was no mission statement of company goals that was related to the "lowly" hourly people on the line. There were lots of slogans on the walls; during nightshift we rearranged them to read like dirty sayings. The list of items goes on forever. You get the picture.

- Other jobs as a young man included working as a draftsman trainee in Grove Manufacturing and later as an inventory clerk in purchasing, a department manager trainee for a large retail firm, a cook in a Mexican food restaurant, a janitor, and a tree trimmer. All of these jobs added to my list of experiences, each with differing managerial styles.

The question quickly becomes "Did I dislike everything? Am I a chronically negative person? Am I a chronic complainer?" No, quite the opposite. The most recurring problem I face in research is to avoid overoptimism in everything. Weren't there any managerial styles I liked overall? All of them were traditional hierarchies. Some more autocratic than others. Yet, within even the most autocratic of the bunch, there were individual foreman and supervisory activities that proved quite positive in obtaining results. This early experience led me to believe progress could be accomplished on a micro-level. That is, by individual supervisors acting and treating workers with respect. By their efforts, they could evoke a positive response in workers that could not otherwise be achieved.

The most unusual incentive I remember occurred while I was a tree trimmer. Our crew worked in a remote mountain area clearing fire lanes and major utility line paths. It is very hot and dirty work in the summer. The foreman was in his mid-thirties and had his work cut out for him. The entire crew was young, ranging in age from sixteen to twenty years old. As a result of doing this work for many years, he knew what we should be able to accomplish in our eight-hour period. He laid out the work first thing in the morning. If we got it done early, there was beer on ice and we could go home early. Well, for a work crew made up of, at that time, under legal drinking age high school and college athletes, the cold beer sounded just fine. The prospect of getting off early and drinking iced beer was a great selection for an incentive plan. We rarely missed our reward that summer.

Now, of course, laws prohibit this kind of incentive, yet the moral of the story is correct. With creativity, we can always find a way to stimulate Golden Rule concepts. Our supervisor followed some of these rules. He treated us like adults: Here is the work, do it and you may leave early. The consequences of working slow were that we had to stay longer. He developed us as a team. It took all of us working together as a unit to leave early; working as individuals we could not finish in time. The consequence of sloppy, low-quality work was that it took longer to complete and accidents resulted. The incentive for success related to the crew's idea of a good reward. Of course, our success was clearly tied to the crew chief's success and to the company's success.

Golden Rule Concepts
- Treat people like adults.
- Let the negative consequences for poor work habits be the workers' choice.
- Show the advantages of working as a team.
- Have the incentives for success be related to the workers' needs.
- Tie the workers' success to the supervisors' success and to the company's goals.

TEACHING THE IDEA

I have spent eleven years in a university setting teaching students these concepts and beliefs about how to handle people. An almost equal number of years were spent as a manager in industry teaching coworkers and subordinates to use the concepts, and, finally, teaching employees and supervisors these concepts as a consultant. I have trained literally thousands of supervisors over the years about the aspects of Golden Rule Management and how to handle people with dignity and respect. Students have included on-the-job workers as well as more traditional college students.

My goal in life for many years has been to deliver the very best classroom experience a student, of any definition, ever had. To achieve this would make me a truly successful person, successful in a sense that a message has positively passed through me to other people who will in turn use and teach, by example, these techniques. That goal remains a part of this book with the reader being the student. The dream was to achieve a snowballing effect by creating believers of the concept of management using the Golden Rule style who would in turn teach others. It is exciting to have students, both corporate and academic, come back and spend hours telling me of their experiences, about what is working and what is not working for them, and about why they didn't think it would work in the beginning. I enjoy hearing about their successes and sharing the joy when they see that this style of treatment can result in positive outcomes beyond their wildest expectations.

I get good marks from students in both the classroom and boardroom. All of us who have been in teaching or training long enough realize there are tricks to the trade. A good colorful speaker with many experiences to draw on can keep students entertained, but the true mark of quality is that the students keep coming back year after year to talk to the newer students coming along and to give their own personal testimonies of success. Another true mark is that they keep coming back and giving me ideas about what to build and how to change and improve and what points they are excited about. These are the people who have gone out to their organizations and tried the process and have become seasoned in the field under fire. They have found the system works. Most people never go back to speak to their former teachers unless they accidentally run into them on the street. For me it is a supreme compliment and an indication that part of my goal is being achieved.

THE GOLDEN RULE IN TRADITIONAL SETTINGS

What about the idea that we're still a rather old-fashioned company? Here I translate "old-fashioned" to mean autocratic or to indicate a company that uses traditional pyramid management structures, both things we are trying to alter significantly. If you work in a traditional environment, does this mean putting this book down right now and going upstairs to get a better night's sleep? The answer is no. Remember my tree crew supervisor? That organization was traditional in structure. Many of the concepts in this book can be implemented irrespective of your boss's management philosophy. Many of the ideas will allow you to see significant success in your own work environment with your own group of employees, success to the point where their lives are enriched by being creative on the job. Your life is enriched by the same sort of creative outlets. Finally, you will be helped by the fact that you are doing your job very well and achieving the expectations your company has set out for you.

How do you know that you can proceed with confidence on this? It's easy for me to say "use these concepts, don't worry about your immediate supervisor." The fact is that in several organizations the concept is already used piecemeal. A little bit here, a little bit there. Some departments went for it, others never were trained in the system. Hershey Chocolate is a very large and successful company with many consultants. During the eleven years I worked with them, we experienced success on a piecemeal basis. At no one time was the whole organization pursuing this program. But, success was achieved in areas where it was used a little bit here, a little bit there. Supervisors who were using Golden Rule Management had the highest praise for its merits. The logical question becomes "Why wasn't it immediately adopted company-wide?" First, I wasn't hired to introduce it company-wide. Second, for the very reasons that affect us all, change is not something we rush into. Plus, this system lacks the flair of a fad. It doesn't have a "one-minute" recipe or a management by objective (MBO)-type plan to follow, and it is geared toward first-line management. Most organizations are ruled from the top down. The concept is so painfully simple, it's overlooked in favor of other solutions. This seems much too easy to work, but it does. The testimony of many first-line supervisors will attest to its merits. This is the first handbook written to serve their needs.

Certainly, you aren't going to be able to do some of the things we will talk about without the whole company buying into the concept. Some of the more radical shifting of policies and procedures that has worked well in other places will need top management support. However, many of the aspects of handling people and the treatment of them can be done without jeopardizing your career. The usual outcome will be that your boss is going to want to know why you are successful and what you have been doing that can be used by other supervisors. Recent surveys of the concerns by top managers reveal that service, product quality, and productivity concerns top the list. If you are able to do something to improve performance, your boss will notice and respond in your favor.

SIMPLICITY IS THE KEY

Golden Rule Management has it origins in some relatively simple philosophies. Some of us may remember back to our early days of studying the Bible. From what I understand from theologians, the Golden Rule is rather consistent across a number of religions. The basic premise is *"Do unto others as you would have them do unto you."* [1] That is, if you wouldn't like to be treated that way, then under no circumstances should you treat an individual that way in the workplace. There is no exception to this. That means if you don't want to be laid off and be without a job and be without food for your family, then don't do that to another individual unless no alternative other than closing down is available. We have enough creative planning and many examples throughout America of companies that have been able to avoid this sort of thing. Laying off someone is a horrid way to treat an individual. It should be a last possible resort *after* we have exhausted our profits, not something we do in order to maintain profit margins. Layoffs are not the only example. The list of ways we treat people poorly in America is rather lengthy. But this book isn't about war stories of negative treatment; let's focus on the positive.

Golden Rule Management: "Do unto others as you would have them do unto you."

For all of us as supervisors this boils down to the key concepts of respect for an individual—respect for them in terms of their self-worth and respect for their status as a valued individual in our organization. We must believe in the dignity of the individual on the job and do what we can to raise, enhance, or maintain the feeling of self-worth and dignity of the individual. People are not a function of their place on an organization chart. In fact, the concept of the traditional pyramid organization becomes rather alien in Golden Rule Management, as you will see as we progress through the philosophy. Our title or rank becomes a rather meaningless term. We all become managers, we all become workers, we all come together, we all become a team. We are hired because of our skills, and we use our skills wherever they are needed in whatever capacity necessary for the success of the organization. At different times and moments, we may be a leader; at a later point, we may be a follower.

Some labor organizations have resisted various Quality of Work Life programs (for example, quality circles, participative management). It is no secret that some companies have used the quality issue and teamwork as a gimic or a quick fix. Other companies have exploited the terminology of

---

[1] St. Matthew 7:12—"What so ever ye would that men should do to you, do ye even so to them."

quality and teams in their advertising without ever incorporating them. Other companies have used team concepts merely to lower labor cost and have ignored the quality of product side of the issue. This kind of experience has been negative for unions. They are hesitant, and rightly so, about further involvement because they fear this may happen again. Golden Rule Management does not encourage or even condone exploitation of workers, which sets this management style apart from schemes to focus on cutting labor costs and thus workers.

Management is not uniquely endowed with superior insight or intelligence because of their function or position as managers. A gray flannel suit image of a boss is not what we are talking about. We are not talking about power ties, power colors, power walking, power sitting, power eating, power riding, power writing, power conversations. We are talking about dealing with whole people and building an emotional bridge to a real person, not a self-constructed, self-image, modeled perhaps after industrial legends or a movie or TV show character.

Work can be one of the most creative opportunities of our lives. The goal of Golden Rule Management is to describe ways we as supervisors, managers, or leaders can help foster the feeling of creativity and growth among individual workers. To me, a very sad situation is one in which people are spending forty percent or more of their lives involved in working overtime on Saturdays, extra shifts, etc., and find that they get little or no creative satisfaction from the job. What they get is a paycheck and a way to feed their family. These are certainly positive points; the family needs to be fed and clothed. However, the employees look for creative outlets in other areas of life rather than their jobs. Certainly we are not trying to tell people not to look for creativity in other avenues. But for the simple respect and dignity of an individual, it is our obligation to try to find ways for the workplace to be a creative outlet for the individual. When we can achieve this level of dignity for a worker, productivity problems simply start to fall by the wayside and we notice the commitment to the job by the individual worker—the type of commitment that achieves productivity and increases quality. It is what we need to compete in the world market. The result is that everybody gains. The company gains because it has a committed work force producing products with the quality and price necessary to be competitive. Workers gain because of their success. They are being rewarded financially, perhaps better than they were before. They are able to meet goals and dreams they have for their lives and families. Just as important, they are achieving a creative outlet through work, and their lives are being fulfilled. They are not left waiting until retirement when "they can begin to live" and begin to "enjoy" themselves. They can begin to live and enjoy themselves on the job. Of course, as a nation we also gain by achieving a higher level of employment and productivity. In addition, the benefits include better trade balances and other economic effects that are far reaching.

Work can be one of the most creative opportunities of our lives. The goal of Golden Rule Management is to foster this feeling among all workers.

Chapter 3

PRODUCTIVITY AS A PROCESS AND GOLDEN RULE MANAGEMENT PRESCRIPTIONS

Productivity in the American workplace is certainly a word that has been thrown hard in our face. The figures we read in the paper are often grim. It has been a downhill slide for the United States basically since 1969. We have lost our first-place position in world commerce; in fact, in selected areas of commerce, we don't even rank in the top three or four. The largest brokerage firm is Japanese, the biggest banks are Japanese, the biggest land holder in Hawaii is Japanese, the British own many of our businesses, the Germans and Japanese share first place in product quality worldwide.

What is productivity and how do we define this term? For many of us productivity is a living process. It is much more than a matter of mixing the "best" combination of inputs to obtain cost efficient levels of outputs. The generic definition used is some measure of output divided by some level of input. Generally, this measure is labor hours because that is what is available on accurate records. It seems neat, quick, and clean—a simple case of division. Yet this definition can distort what capital and the quality of various management systems can contribute in the company. The generic definition in the traditional setting is efficiency; that is, getting the most output with the smallest amount of input. Remember, the traditional measure is labor hours per some unit of time. That definition means we tend to undervalue interpersonal relationships and the quality and experience of employees within the organizations. The emphasis on interpersonal relationships is often referred to as the "soft" side of management (the "hard" side being output figures). It is only in recent years that emphasis on the soft side of management is being recognized as equally important to the success of an organization.

On many international fronts confusion exists. Our executives grasp at every management fad that comes along. It is kind of frightening for us that even the marketing geniuses of this country for many years could not even sell their own companies on the need to put the steering wheel on the other side of the car in order to sell it in Japan. Nor can they convince them to make washers, dryers, and refrigerators that run on different currents and will fit into the homes of our foreign competitors. It's no wonder that in the United States we are stuck with forest and agricultural products as our chief exports. "Stuck" in that there is such a small percentage of total employment involved in these areas that the net effect for us as a nation is minimal.

Golden Rule Management is going to challenge some managerial myths. We are going to challenge a few of the former "tried and true" myths. We are going to look at a simple plan that can help us change many of our problems with productivity, a plan that has been used with success for more than a decade now by some of the biggest corporations in America. It has also been used with success by some very tiny corporations and in production line situations, banks, high-tech organizations, and service companies. You see, all that we need to succeed is basically present. We just have to capture the spirit of what can be achieved and do it.

To do it, we use a phrase basic to some people from when they were children in Sunday School, when the Golden Rule was taught: "Do unto others as you would like done unto you" (St. Matthew 7:12). A remarkably simple phrase, yet, at times so very hard for us to carry out. We have translated this for our use to read Golden Rule Management.

ADULT-LIKE TREATMENT

Adult-like treatment begins with the premise of respect and dignity for workers, with a belief that your workers are good, and your workers want to do their jobs. The glue that holds this premise together is mutual good faith between a manager and a worker. This premise rarely exists, yet, virtually every top manager claims to be using the ideas of adult-like treatment in their organizations.

I do not claim to be the first to notice this gap in treatment between what a manager claims in a positive note and what workers perceive as a negative reality. Chris Argyris wrote in 1957 of the conflict between workers and the bureaucratic system. It was, according to Argyris (1957), to the benefit of the organization to keep workers from achieving a sense of maturity, self-awareness, independence, and equality. If organizations are able to keep workers passive, dependent, and limited in behavior, then the illusion of control by managers could be maintained. This illusion of control and predictability incorrectly gives the idea that such a worker attitude will result in lower costs. Lower costs are, of course, the direct route to bottom-line thinking. This focus on the bottom line, almost to the exclusion of quality and other legitimate business goals, has resulted in a short-term mentality that hurts our competitive efforts.

Argyris goes on to indicate that this failure to enhance adult-like treatment of workers and the focus on the bottom line produces feelings of alienation, low motivation, and dissatisfaction in many workers. This attitude in the workers leads management to try to remedy the problem of low motivation and dissatisfaction by applying even greater levels of control over the worker. This becomes a no-win situation that results in a basic philosophical difference between workers and the organization under our traditional management style. This doesn't have to be the case. Golden Rule Management has a different set of assumptions about control.

People want to be treated as adults. That is basically what we are talking about when we use respect and dignity. We want to be treated like an adult on the job, not someone's handmaiden, servant, or child. This is not a unique concept. Students in adult learning have been calling for this for years. Even texts from the 1940s mention it. Yet the signs of our failure to actually see the words or hear the cry for dignity are everywhere. Respect, dignity, and adult treatment are not present where:

- Time clocks are used

- Buzzers or bells sound to make the workers salivate for their lunch

- Reserved parking designates the status of the person in the organization

- Supervisors wear different colored hats or clothing to denote status

- Manager's paychecks arrive in envelopes and workers' checks are handed out without being properly sealed.

This list could go on, but I think you get the idea of the type of things that we do to workers that we wouldn't want done to us. Doing so creates a gulf between us. It doesn't create a partnership or team with a sense of camaraderie, which is what we need to achieve our goals. By achieving these goals for ourselves, our organization, and our nation, we will be able to return to our state of prosperity. The above concepts are worthwhile irrespective of the organization. This is not a concept that is too vague or narrow in scope for manufacturing, service, retail, government, or other entities.

THE CONDITION OF MANUFACTURING

Quality management concepts often appear to be targeted to manufacturing. To many people, there is little left to save in manufacturing. We won't get lost in a tangent here, but the United States, according to a lot of people, is virtually out of the manufacturing business. I did some checking on this, and startling as it may seem, right now there are more people employed in manufacturing in America than at any time in our history.[2] This surprises a lot of people and frequent reactions are "People tell me differently," "But I heard it on TV," "I read it in the paper," or "We're a service economy, aren't we?" There is also a lot of negative gloom and doom about all the industries that are failing, about the quality of our products that can't compete. Stories abound about the fact that there is no more small appliance manufacturing in America. The list goes on and on. Certainly there is some redistribution of people. Some industries have fallen into very bad times, and it looks as if others are going to have the same redistribution and some more failures will occur. Part of this can be attributed to international trade and currency difficulties, to poor management, to the life cycle of products, and to the failure of companies to realize and keep a proper definition of the type of business in which they are involved.

But despite these problems, right now more people are engaged in manufacturing than ever before. To compound the confusion here, we don't know how to classify modern manufacturing. You see, we seem to need high levels of noise and pollution to be satisfied that manufacturing is taking place. But, if we create an idea, that is a manufacturing process, not a service. We call just about everything that we don't know what to call, "service." That is incorrect. The United States has been referred to as a chief exporter of ideas. According to what I have been able to figure out, we are still the top creative nation in the world. In some regards the nature of manufacturing has shifted sharply in America and perhaps changed for the better. This transition to high-tech idea manufacturing is causing our secondary and vocational education sectors to be in a state of transition trying to adjust to the new demands for skills. The very labor-intensive, dirty, and unsafe jobs may be carried on by developing economies where they are willing to trade off their environment. For example, the only steel production to speak of in America that appears to be competitive, is in mini steel plants and specialty steel plants. Our manufacturing is transforming into

[2] For an expanded discussion of this topic, the reader may turn to Robert Z. Lawrence "Is Deindustrialization a Myth?" in Staudohas and Brown (1987).

more high-tech R&D facilities and the like.[3] Is that all bad? In these areas, the skills of the worker are more fully utilized and jobs seems to be more satisfying to the worker.

DO WE TRADE IN OUR WORKERS?

The U.S. worker—is he or she any good? Are they worth saving? I don't know how many seminars I have attended in which a slide on the wall extols the virtues of a Japanese worker. Somehow they want to take our people and create something different. Well, that doesn't have to be. This may challenge yet another myth, but our workers are still among the most productive people in the world. To challenge another, our workers are not the most expensive in hourly wages. The figures show that we rank somewhere around fifth, maybe down to eighth or tenth, depending on the industry. When I was doing research for a book I coauthored about employee benefits, I ran across numerous examples of countries that had more benefits than the United States. Germans have more extensive vacations from their first day on the job, they have higher benefits, and they are paid more overall. So are Belgian workers, and in many cases so are the British.[4] The Germans have a competitive edge on the United States. They produce more goods and services than we do. Yet, with their higher labor and benefit costs and more time away from the job on vacations we should have the edge! Apparently, there is more to achieving high productivity and winning trade wars than mere labor cost differentials![5]

That makes it even more confusing as to why companies run to Mexico for production when Mexico doesn't rank in the top group in terms of output per person-day. It is very confusing. Figures don't necessarily support running to such a nation to build your product. We have productive workers here. They can do the job. What we need is for them to be managed more professionally in order to be competitive and to achieve the levels of output that are necessary.

The best workers in the world are right here in our businesses, yours and mine. However, we don't let them work. We hire them from the neck

---

[3] The reader is referred to Robert Z. Lawrence, "Is Deindustrialization a Myth?" in Staudohas and Brown (1987) for a more technical discussion on this topic.

[4] The Democratic National Convention of 1992 made America aware of the differentials with foreign competition. For a more detailed discussion of this, the reader is referred to Peter J. Dowling and Randall Schuler, *International Dimensions Human Resource Management*, PWS-Kent Publishing, Boston. Wage and benefit data are available from the Bureau of Labor Statistics or in any number of basic labor economics and labor relations books.

[5] For an expanded discussion on this topic, the reader is directed to Holoviak and Sipkoff (1987, pp. 3–11) and Holoviak (1984a, pp. 1–3).

down and we avoid the brain. We have supervisors and quality control people looking over their shoulders at virtually every turn. "We need them," you say! If we trust and believe in our people, then both of these management types are unnecessary to the extent that they are currently used in American industry. The giant candy producer, H. B. Reese Company, put quality where it belongs, with their employees on the assembly line who make the product. They have changed quality control in the traditional sense and put it back on the assembly line with the individuals, who make sure that the candy has the proper amount of candy in the cup and that the wrappers are tightly sealed, etc. The result has been a constant increase in overall quality and a decrease in customer complaints due to quality. Not having supervisors looking over our shoulder is a dream of many employees who have launched into semi-autonomous work groups. The creed of these employers reads:

> "We hired you Mr./Ms. Employee because of your skills and your brains. Now we trust you to do the work. We are going to treat you like an adult."

Here are some results from companies who have cut back on the number and closeness of supervision:

- Increased output
- Decreased turnover in employees
- Increased employee job satisfaction.

This is not new. It goes back to the 1980 experiments of the Bolivar study of the GM plant where it was tried. A number of companies have tried similar experiments. A quick look through the literature of quality of work life, which touched on some of these issues, confirms this. In the Bolivar study, the techniques achieved tremendous success; the confusion is why GM didn't proceed with the idea in virtually every plant and every other job setting right away. Other companies have gone forward with very positive results. Hershey Chocolate Company, Telecommunications Product Corporation, Rohr Industries, and Certain Teed Corporation are just a few of the many who have tried varying degrees of participative programs. Some attempts have been used with success and some did not work as expected.

Chapter 4

THE TEAMING PROCESS AND THE GOLDEN RULE

More than ten years of practice in forming teams in organizations has taught me a number of lessons. The first lesson is that, irrespective of type of business, people are the same. Oh, they may have more education, maybe they are more technical, but their behavioral reactions are similar. I have, with various coresearchers in different cases, tracked results for more than a decade. The behavioral factors are numerous; the output results and cost savings were tracked as well. In fact, some of the research published was the first in the field to be technically analyzed. It is published in professional journals, academic journals, conference proceedings, and working papers. The results are published in technical writing that I believe few people have understood or even read because it looked boring. As such, this explanation, as is true of the rest of this book, is not technical but operational.

What is the connection of teams to Golden Rule Management? Why bring it up? Team building fits comfortably in the process. Its goals are a fuller utilization of employee talents and greater autonomy for them. Greater autonomy means a reduced need for layers of management. Besides more profits, the work has been systematically redistributed so that the reduction in managerial ranks does not leave a void in task completion or overwork those who remain.

Team building and employee participation often happen in stages. The process often begins with suggestion boxes or systems. Frequently, these are not overwhelmingly successful. The focus is on big savings issues and fails to involve employees. Few people fill out suggestions for small items. The next step is quality circle-type programs. The key point at this step may be the volunteer nature of many quality circles and the large amount of management control over topics approached. Yet, where implemented properly, quality circles have been a positive force in productivity and quality and lead to the next step in the teaming process.

The next phase is task teams. Now, these can be instituted before quality circles or even suggestion boxes, however, we often see them at this step in the progression. Task teams generally originate from managers. They decide the issues, usually big dollar items. The teams include all levels of workers and their team life is as long as the problem takes to be solved. These task teams are dedicated to the project and generate excitement from the participants. However, their existence depends on management starting up new task groups. The workers lack power to initiate or maintain the programs.

Semi-autonomous work groups are the next step in the evolution of *Teaming*, which is what the whole process is generically called. It is characterized by a lack of traditional supervisors and their influence. This is the aspect of "quality circles" the Japanese, Swedes, and Germans have perfected. Let's clarify a point here. People working in groups is not teaming, but it does become teaming when they assume more control of the process. Such things as quality control, the amount of production, and how to handle the job, even to the extent of deciding vacations or hiring, fit the transition. The commitment to the company and job is very strong. Employees have a voice in many aspects of running the organization. Once set in place, this becomes such a satisfying mode of work that it would take years to "get rid" of this level of participation if the organization so decided. Employees would not easily surrender this feeling of commitment.

> People working in groups is not teaming. It becomes teaming when the workers assume control of the process.

The final step in teaming moves us to the point at which the typical pyramid structure is difficult to keep and is replaced by more fluid designs that more aptly suit employee skills and the nature of the product or service. A myth often heard about teaming is that it will lack accountability. True traditionalists of the pyramid structure feel they can identify that "one person" who is responsible. Well, it was surprising for me to learn over the years that accountability is enhanced with teaming. The level of responsibility of each person is increased, meaning we all are held responsible for our projects or products. Our fate is not left to one person's ability. If one person goofs, it affects us all. In teaming, we agree to the decision by consensus and are all participants in the progress. In times of stress, people often wish to defer responsibility back to one person. My experience with first-line supervisors shows that they fear teams because they are afraid of not being able to tell their boss "who goofed." They later learn that who goofed doesn't really matter.

Each case of teaming is different; there is no one "blueprint" for doing it right. We must take into account the culture of our own organization and arrange the system to satisfy these particulars. For example, the Hershey Corporation has a long history and well-entrenched culture. Several generations in the same family commonly work for the company. The shift to teaming takes time and energy and understanding on behalf of management. A new company has less trouble because there are few traditions in jeopardy. That means we use our "heads" and "instinct." You must be the "salesperson" and coach for teams.

FAMILY TIES

Forming a team is a lot like building a strong family relationship. The end result of a strong family is a close bond of members with high affiliation, affection, loyalty, and intrinsic (coming from inside one) motivation to support the family unit. But the road to that point is no cake walk. It is achieved by hard, often frustrating work.

When members of a family gather under a single roof only to sleep or eat the feeling of being family is absent. When each family member concentrates solely on doing his or her own thing, without regard to family wishes, the feeling and rewards of family are absent. Family building involves give and take on the part of each person toward the shared vision of the family goals.

Frequently family members resist family goals. Teenagers reject parental values. Individual members do not contribute to the work of running the house. A lot of effort is necessary to redirect their energies and focus toward family values, just as the supervisor must refocus team member energies. Certainly, we can reject the difficult member; we can argue, fight, or avoid the person. But the result is intense stress on the whole unit and a lack of a unified group pursuing their goals.

Neither is it a family if all the sacrifice comes at the expense of one or two members. This is not to say mom or dad doesn't do the bulk of the work. However, if mom is serving as chauffeur, housekeeper, cook, PTA representative, den mother, and Sunday School teacher, what are the others giving to be sure mom has a chance to grow? If dad is gardener, scout master, plummer, etc., and has no time to "grow," is this a family unit? In neither case here would the unit be a family or a team.

If team success is based on the energy of one or two members, it is not balanced. The success of teams, like families, means we all must contribute.

If one or two employees do it all and other team members are not contributing to success, then they are not learning the necessary team values. Having someone else "take" all the time for your success is the self-centered format in which our organizations currently operate. Top managers reap the glory and pay while legions of workers produce. Are we advocating that parents abandon their children's piano lessons and gym classes? Obviously not, but a family whose cohesiveness is not balanced is not a shared unit of cohesive energy. Similarly, we are indicating that we cannot refer to a group of workers as a team if its survival is dependent on just the supervisor's energy.

Family units also involve shared decision-making. Absolute control over family members will usually result in rebellious children in their teens. Does this mean mom and dad have no say? Not necessarily. There is no question who heads up the family, but facilitative control yields an atmosphere of confidence and growth in all family members. The same is true for workers. There is a library full of evidence that autocratic control of employees results in negative behavior. Change is difficult, but we can break this cycle.

Perhaps the major complaint I have recorded over the past decade from major corporations is the time factor involved in using this management style. In the beginning teams seem to take up too much time. Members claim they are always at meetings! "I can't do my work because of attending meetings" is a cry often heard. With proper time-management skills and meeting management training, this claim quickly goes away. That sentence sounds easy, but it means taking time away from the job and learning these skills. Plus, it takes time to convince people that the work is the meeting. Yes, you read correctly. That returning to their desks or production line is the means to carry out the decisions of the group. Meetings decide critical alternatives to "What if" scenarios ahead of time. Plus, they provide continuous valuable information about the organization and a chance for employee input to be heard.

Teaming produces fears among supervisors. Supervisors fear cross-trained, well-informed, and motivated groups will make their jobs unnecessary. The goal is certainly to streamline organizations and reduce layers of management, but nothing happens overnight. If properly moved along, normal attrition combined with organizational growth may well take care of the problem. Supervisors are needed, but it is the direction of their emphasis that changes. Some parents do feel threatened by children who are self-sufficient, but they are rare; most delight in watching family members grow in stature and confidence. We became supervisors to facilitate people's growth. Teaming helps free supervisors to do this most important part of the job.

> Teaming frees the supervisor to become a facilitator of employee growth.

Team building requires constant attention. We need to direct our supervisors' efforts to the facilitation of people. I have been involved in this process with steel mills, hospitals, high-tech companies, sales/marketing companies, banks, candy companies, farm equipment manufacturers, and government agencies to varying degrees for more than a decade. My early research in organization structure dates back more than thirteen years. Make no mistake, this change should not be considered on a whim or as a patchwork idea. It takes time, energy, and money to be done on an organization-wide basis. It is a major change in philosophy. Even in circumstances where supervisors are incorporating these ideas separate from a company-wide effort, the change is not immediate. It will take a concerted effort to succeed, but the results are worth it.

A positive side effect of treating workers as adults comes from increased profits and managerial efficiency. The decrease in output in U.S. industries is not to be laid solely at the feet of our workers. Let's look at Sears as an example. Twenty-five years ago in business schools, Sears was pointed out as a model of managerial efficiency. Now it seems to be an overburdened corporation with too many layers of management. Ford Corporation, with too many layers of management at the factory level, couldn't get the type of decisions they needed to enhance product quality. Many organizations have realized they have too many layers of management and are streamlining their operations.

Ladies and gentlemen, in my opinion it does not matter what you try to cut in both production and labor costs, you cannot cut enough with the excess managerial overhead and staff that we have in many American organizations. We don't need so many managers. We have good workers. Let's allow them to work, think, and meet the challenge as a team to produce the product—produce it with quality for a price at which we can sell it.

Unfortunately, we tend to try to streamline our organizations by simply removing layers of people. In short-term accounting this works, but in the long term it fails. It's like a fad diet. We lose pounds quickly, then we resume our old behaviors and return to our former weight. Streamlining an organization involves careful redesign of an organization, redesigning of jobs into defined skill areas so that the work still gets done efficiently. Eliminating layers, on the other hand, means work is shoved up or down to someone who may not have the appropriate skills. The long-term result is an inefficient handling of work, frustrated workers, and lower productivity. Of course, simply eliminating layers of management by firing lacks the level of dignity a worker deserves. There are better ways to achieve streamlined results.

PRACTICING WHAT YOU PREACH

For more than a decade I had the privilege of being the director of the successful H. R. Frehn Center of Management at Shippensburg University in Shippensburg, Pennsylvania. This unit serves as the outreach arm of the College of Business, and its activities are diverse. They include a small business center, a government training center, computer training, artificial intelligence work, direct consulting activities, research publications, and various grant-related activities.

Yet, it wasn't always this way. The center was a small one-person operation from 1976 to 1980. The emphasis changed in 1980. The dean of the College of Business envisioned a more active role for the university in our research activities. The problem was in finding creative ways to grow without upfront monetary university support. As is the case with many small state universities, there is no money to put "at risk" or upfront to sponsor such growth. Our activities had to be internally funded. This, of course, could have been viewed in the negative. On the other hand, it could be looked at as an opportunity to try out new ideas right under my nose. So, the Frehn Center began as a semi-autonomous work setting. Those familiar with state bureaucracies realize this was no easy task. It was difficult coping with the state's narrow job descriptions and rigid titles to allow flexibility in the use of personnel.

The center was set up as a one-person, one-vote system. That is, when we had our meetings, if a center employee wanted to pursue a new area of business, he or she prepared a proposal and it was reviewed and a vote taken. The director did not have veto power. My job was facilitator of staff talents. I worked for consensus, along with everyone else.

The proposals were business plans. The process was making business people out of employees—employees capable of making sound decisions based on facts of cost and revenue. Of course, this made the tie in to organization goals much easier. What is important here is that they were state workers who typically did not make decisions from this bottom-line perspective.

This model could be very helpful in these times of tight state budgets. On the surface this management style seems to be loose and maybe courting chaos. But the opposite has resulted. It has fostered countless areas of creativity balanced by employee judgment as to what is realistic. Areas of business I envisioned as weak, and would have otherwise vetoed, have worked out brilliantly. For example, such areas as remote satellite training systems and software training and design were center areas of expertise long before they were heard of by the general public.

It is easy to remember those first meetings. Yes, it was hard not to assume an authority role. My compassion for managers who have spent their lives in traditional settings, and now must change, is genuine. It is hard not to jump in and solve issues. My feelings were strong. To borrow and set up a very expensive computer lab to train people seemed risky at best. The same was true of many new areas of business, but the exhilaration in the eyes of the staff that first time will stay forever in my mind. None of them had ever experienced this level of decentralization and empowerment before. For that matter my experience at this level of empowerment was thin. It was always a dream to have this kind of feeling on the job. It was how I always wished my talents could be used. As the Golden Rule implies, if you wish to be treated that way, then you must treat others in the same fashion. It was a leap of faith and trust for us all. Ten years later the exhilaration and creativity among the staff continue.

Then and now, people are hired because of skills and may pursue career paths that in some cases will result in their leaving the center to work elsewhere. Before leaving, they are excited about work and see a clear path to their career goals. After they leave, room becomes available for others who wish to move along to new skill areas. Just because the primary skill area may be secretarial in nature would not preclude that employee from leading a program as well. The use of narrow job parameters can kill enthusiasm. An employee can have talents in many areas. The center lets these talents emerge. The idea is to count on people wanting to do more. The state regularly has "complement" requirements, that is, limits on the number of employees who can be employed, which means more staff cannot readily be hired despite the ability to pay or level of need. The effect is an excited, creative, and committed work force.

Since the center does not receive much university support in terms of money, their creativity must include the practical aspect of paying salaries, purchasing equipment and supplies, and having upfront resources to pursue new avenues of work. As part of a state university it cannot pursue avenues of business that directly compete with private concerns. The compound effect is to be faced continuously with the necessity of developing new lines of business that are on the cutting edge. This can be from computer-type high-tech areas to the wide range of human resource developmentment training. The semi-autonomous work setting (empowerment) provides this atmosphere. Empowerment means there are virtually no internal constraints such as:

- Hours required to work or time cards
- Narrow job descriptions
- Titles that restrict creativity
- Strictly defined work roles
- Dress codes
- Status definitions of office size, etc.

Empowerment means setting people free to use their full potential, free of unnecessary rules or supervisory oversight. It means treating people as you wish to be treated—like adults who can act responsibly and who can do good work on their own. Empowerment creates people who act and perform as if they have a vested interest in the organization, even when the job is at a government agency like the Frehn Center.

However, there are state requirements of a narrow nature, and the center did comply with all filing requirements, but hard work is necessary if we are to fulfill these requirements without resorting to threats or negative practices. To do so would destroy the creative atmosphere of the center. Certainly, to be this creative in a state bureaucracy within a university bureaucracy requires support. Our dean showed support of our nontraditional mode of operations and philosophically endorsed the concept of decentralized work groups.

The staff was free to select their own work hours. Everyone knows what type of staffing is necessary to cover phones, etc., and this includes the director and the person who is the "official" assistant director. Status perks like fancy offices are generally ignored. When I was director, my office was used by anyone who needed it. It was the quick way to get from one side of the work area to the other. As such, it was also a thoroughfare.

Status perks distort the focus of employee attention from the goals of the organization. Achieving a perk becomes the employee focus. Retaining the perk means status differences are reinforced. In the center there is virtually no fixed skill areas by rank. That is, on Tuesday and Thursday the employee may perform receptionist-secretarial duties and on Monday and Wednesday he or she may be off consulting with a client. Friday may see the employee participating in a board of directors meeting at some local organization. This diversity is encouraged for those who wish to pursue personal/career growth in this manner.

Much has been learned from the activities of the Frehn Center about how semi-autonomous groups interact. For example, it takes time to be self-generating. In fact, years of time. I compare it to fire retardant materials. They will burn as long as heat is applied; when heat is withdrawn they quit burning. The same applies here. As long as there is a constant source of energy flowing to keep the groups going, it works. You can't send people to training or certification programs and expect the semi-autonomous program to run itself from that point on. It took five years of energy and constant reminders of how the concept flows to achieve the self-generating effects. That is, when the heat source was removed, the fire kept burning by itself. Some things we have learned don't vary with the culture. For example, no amount of worker self-control over their working lives replaces the desire for certain levels of income and health protection insurance.

During the early years, in times of a major crisis, project managers assume more control, and the consensus form of decision-making was not always followed as closely, although it was not abandoned. This was an area of some concern at first. Yet, during the decade several major crises occurred, and, after they had passed, the team members asserted themselves quickly to regain control. They have an advantage here. Everyone around them in the university is in rather rigid job areas and a traditional structure. No one on the staff wants to end up in that arrangement and lose the autonomy they have grown to enjoy. As they matured in the process, they began to handle crises as a group with consensus.

By comparison, client organizations where the center works do not have the constant inspiration of seeing how it "could be worse." For them, it is not uncommon to have people back peddle to old styles of interaction. The input of energy must be constant. The vision of what is to be achieved must continually be reinforced and discussed.

> It is not uncommon to back peddle to old styles of interactions. The input of energy must always be present. Someone must continually reinforce and discuss the vision of what is to be achieved.

Finally, it must be mentioned that our center is unionized. The staff is divided among three separate unions. Potentially this could be a disaster. Two of the three unions are not vocal supporters of cooperative systems and the third is neutral. The Golden Rule concept strongly reinforces worker autonomy and respect, both of which are basic tenets of unions.

It is no secret that many unions openly oppose any form of cooperation as a sham for exploitation. In the defense of these unions, some forms of cooperation are just work speedup shams. True worker cooperatives stress the eventual evolutionary trail leading to an autonomous worker in charge of his or her own work environment. The entire program at our center is an ongoing, ever-changing process of employee growth and development. It fits with the union movement and thus offers no reason for conflict.

But this experience at the center has served to reinforce the Golden Rule concept in an organization's structure and operation. It serves as an ongoing laboratory to observe firsthand the evolutionary aspects of this process. It is also a legitimate way to tell people that, yes, I have used the system. I lived with it daily for more than a decade and found it personally rewarding and organizationally efficient.

Teamwork has many challenges, including (at times) the courts and the National Labor Relations Board (NLRB). An NLRB ruling in late 1992 added a new challenge to the issue of unions setting participative programs by holding that an Indiana-based firm illegally dominated manager—worker committees (Wall Street Journal, December 12, 1992). This decision is narrowly worded. Most experts feel it will not stop this process, but it will be in the courts for some time. The court action can be positive. This kind of close attention will keep the process of teaming democratic and may stop the public relations show of teams in our organizations.

Chapter 5

ONE-TO-ONE

The result would be both pleasant, effective, and efficient if a company's management philosophy were consistent and evenly dispersed throughout the upper and lower levels of the organization. From most appearances, such conditions are rare. Even in those companies whose public relations staff verbally endorses and recommends this philosophy, one often encounters contradictory work practices and policies. We often find top management boastfully exclaiming to be total quality oriented, team managed, or "quality-circled." However, the practice is usually lost at the midlevel of management and rarely filters down to the bottom. It's not unusual to hear top management demanding everyone to be team oriented, while they practice a managerial style characterized by dictates and autocratic behavior.

As an expert in training first-line to midlevel managers, I frequently encounter scenarios where the top people want "something done for that group." It would be better if they would practice Golden Rule concepts themselves. However, considerable progress can still be made and help offered if the front-line levels are going it alone.

That is what this chapter is about: achieving new levels of efficiency for yourself, ushering in new ways of positive employee treatment that will result in increasing the dignity and self-esteem of each person supervised. After all, when all is said and done, that is what we are hired to do. We are not hired to lament the reasons our senior staff fail to practice good management techniques. We are not hired to use past attempts at change that failed as excuses for not going forward now. We cannot let their actions be an ongoing excuse for our not changing and doing things differently. Your adoption of the Golden Rule process may well be the catalyst that sparks others to try it. One person *can* make a difference.

MEETING PEOPLE WHERE THEY ARE

The first step in using Golden Rule Management is to "meet" people where they are. This doesn't necessarily imply a physical location, although at times that is helpful. What I mean is to meet them on their mental and emotional ground. Expecting others to come to where and what you are thinking is unrealistic.

Case Example

The organization has said that supervisors will use team practices and involve the employees more. All the supervisors were trained in the technical aspects of team problem solving, methods of involvement, and various quality circle points. Yet, there is no involvement, the employees reject the idea and refuse to be part of the process.

The typical response to this situation is to begin arm twisting and threats. If that does not produce results, we then move to disciplinary actions. Both are one-way models of communication where authority flows from the top down. We fully expect the employees to buy into the concept. In fact, it may anger our senior staff that the employees don't appreciate what is being done for them. After all, they are being given a chance to have a say!

Yet, no one has taken into account the emotional side of the employee. No one has formed employee focus groups to seek out why they don't participate. This scenario is a real one and is very common. When we meet the people where they are, we find some common responses for their resistance. Examples of these responses follow:

- "This is just another fad, it will go away like the others. Then, I am left as an employee excited and committed to a concept the top managers are bored with and no longer endorse. I don't need that emotional roller coaster again."

- "I do not know how to participate. The whole time I've worked here nobody asked me a thing. When I did speak up in the past either I was told to be quiet or nothing happened. You trained the supervisors, why not train me as an employee to know how to participate."

- "If the organization gets all these new efficiencies claimed by teamwork, what happens to me. Top management gets a bonus while at the same time I get laid off since there won't be a need for so many workers! How does this help me?"

- "The only participation that top management wants to hear is what saves money now. It doesn't matter if it makes the job better for the workers, which will eventually make it more efficient. If it doesn't save labor cost, we never see our idea used!"

The list of employee responses is lengthy. The point is well made by the employees. We expect this participation and loyalty, yet we don't address their concerns or try to make the change a positive program for them. A common top management response puts faith in the idea of better job security through participation. The idea of job security becomes a threat. Yes, it's that plain and simple. Telling them it keeps the organization profitable, which guarantees job security, is perceived as a threat. No one likes to live or work under a threat. This is not to say the top managers are really threatening people. The articulation of the idea among top managers is clear: becoming more efficient through participation will benefit everyone. However, the articulation of this often becomes less precise as the message makes its way down the chain of command. It loses the feeling of community and sounds more like a system purge.

Another common problem is the institution of technical change. Newer and more up-to-date equipment means doing more work with less people. The responses include passive resistance strategies, in which the bare minimum is achieved, more direct resistance in not "getting" the hang of the new equipment, or outright sabotage of the new equipment.

> Selling participative techniques to workers by using job security as the bait is perceived as a threat. No one likes to live or work under a threat. Be careful about how you transmit the vision across the organization.

In the preceding scenario the failure was in not dealing with people where they were mentally and emotionally. There are some things that can be done one-on-one with your employees:

- Emotional bridges
- Straight talk
- Face-to-face techniques.

Before these techniques are explained, let me mention something else. These techniques are not intended to be the last word in dealing with people. This book is not just an exercise in practical "how to" techniques. How to do it is the easy part. The mental frame of reference or state of mind is the key. There are literally dozens of "how to" books on the market. In the university settings, through various consulting organizations, and adult education, instruction in how to do it has been available for years. What has been lacking is the balance, the balance that takes the applied mechanics and turns it into a workable program. Many quality programs are very strong on measurement and statistics but fail to balance with interpersonal skills.

The approach used here has been taught to many supervisors at all levels in organizations. In addition, many hourly people have been taught the Golden Rule techniques of personal interaction. In modern organizations where leadership is not a function of "official title" but is part of our everyday life, such skills are essential for all workers. The concepts used here have early roots in the literature on behavioral psychology. Sharon, my wife and training partner, and I have spent years working on and modifying the concept implementation.

EMOTIONAL BRIDGES

The "emotional bridges" technique of handling people is very useful. Plus, it has strong intuitive appeal that makes it feel "natural" for supervisors. It combines the elements of empathy and positivism into a technique of proactive interaction with an employee.

Steps in the Emotional Bridges Approach

- Start your talk by pointing out the employee's positive contributions.
- Ask the person for his or her feelings or confirm your understanding of those feelings.
- Then you take into account the other person's feelings, dealing with the specific points you wish to talk about.
- Finally, your supervisory position on the specific issues must be explained again.

This technique is an assertive or proactive technique to correct a work situation that is not satisfactory. The points that make it successful are the positive beginning to bolster self-esteem. That is followed by building the emotional bridge through using words that reflect our understanding of both the workers feelings and the actual problem.

Case Example

In a small regional bank, the majority of the customer contact employees are female and the management staff is male. This is certainly not an unusual circumstance. However, changing demographics, education levels, and the economy have made it more difficult to recruit and retain tellers, specifically, and bank employees, in general. The staff is unwilling to tolerate the treatment and low pay that in prior years was found to be acceptable. The female staff believe the male supervisors have no real understanding of their problems with child care, elder care, and expanded work demands. The recent management demand was increasing work hours, which made it difficult to deal with babysitters and related family matters.

The male managers insist they do understand. Obviously, there is a problem. The men claim they hear what the female tellers are saying, yet the female staff is quite confident they do not.

We taught the emotional bridges approach to all supervisors, but focused on this group that was encountering difficulty. The male supervisors' subsequent ability to project empathy made a difference. The proper tone of voice and selection of words that reflected to the tellers the very rough position they were placed in was finally "listened" to by their supervisors.

This doesn't mean the tellers ran off to work the longer hours with a smile, but it did produce a successful communication for both parties. This success reduced the hostilities, which makes for better customer relations, fewer errors, and better attendance. Of similar importance, it fosters a bond between worker and supervisor that establishes a basis for mutual decision-making and problem solving in the future.

STRAIGHT TALK

The roots of straight talk lie in the premise of being treated as you would wish to be treated. This technique describes the feelings of the supervisor about the continued actions by a worker that are unacceptable. There is no dodging of the issue or hiding behind "policy" or "rules" when addressing the person. The supervisor will be directly relating worker behavior to his or her feelings and the negative effect it is having on the supervisor. Again, the focus is on the behavior of the person, not his or her personality or being. Nor are we attacking the person in an aggressive fashion.

Steps in the Straight Talk Approach

- The conversation starts by telling the worker what you see as the problem and is put in objective terms such as time spent, money lost, or customers annoyed.

- Next, and the key to this approach, you relate the behavior or problem to how it makes you feel, to how it negatively affects you and your own feelings.

- Ask the employee for ideas about how to resolve the situation. Even if you can't use the suggestion, perhaps you can "piggyback" on part of it. Use some of the employee's idea, some of yours. It may be a springboard to a new solution.

- In specific terms, relate back to the person what you need him or her to do. Not just a policy requirement type statement, but what you need changed in terms of behavior.

When you use this technique, the employee often desires to comment. Allow for this and don't be afraid to reply. This dialogue will further clarify the changes you need to have accomplished. For some employees it may be their first emotion-based encounter with you or any manager. Use active listening techniques to help them. That is, use an open body posture and lean forward to encourage their comments. Be careful not to interrupt, but paraphrase back to the person the content and feelings of their message. This technique is a very balanced approach for both the employee and the supervisor. For the employee we are being empathetic and at the same time assertive. For the manager, he or she is balancing being a real person by expressing emotions, not hiding behind organizational rules, policies, or similar actions that are cold and dry.

Case Example

A state agency is trying to engage the nonexempt work force in the total quality approach to participative management. The supervisors have received training in the methods of involvement, yet the nonexempt employees do not subscribe to this change and will not participate.

This is not an uncommon problem in today's budget-cutting environment. Many public sector organizations are scurrying to make the necessary changes for survival. For a number of valid reasons, the employees fail to participate.

The straight talk technique helps balance the cold, often matter-of-fact approach that our top managers often take to pursue change. It lets employees know that their resistance hurts more than the company; it hurts them as the supervisor. It spells out how the supervisor feels and brings out in clear language what is needed. Straight talk includes the employee viewpoint where possible. Even if you can't use it, it shows respect for the individual. You as the supervisor recognized they had an opinion and allowed them to express it.

FACE-TO-FACE TECHNIQUE

The face-to-face technique implies that there is a more serious behavior we must deal with, typically a recurring type of situation where we have previously spoken with the person and have received no real behavioral changes. The most difficult point in using this technique is to avoid becoming aggressive. When we confront and become aggressive, a win or lose situation is created. This means the loss of self-esteem and dignity, followed closely by output efficiency and quality. Remember, you or I would not want to be directly approached in an aggressive manner. Therefore, don't use such an approach with another person.

Steps in the Face-to-Face Approach

- Begin by summarizing past meetings and agreements not kept.
- Next, describe in clear and precise wording what has to be changed.
- Again, in a nonaccusatory fashion, tell the person how you see his or her behavior and the variance from the expected.
- In precise terms, layout what the person must do.

Face-to-Face Example

"You and I spoke several times before about how cash-in's would be handled at the teller's window. We agreed to how it would be done. I notice you are still handling them the old way. I need you to change to the new procedure immediately. Our audit and accounting procedures are based on the new system."

Face-to-Face Example

"Your travel expense reports are not being filled out as we agreed. You are not including the correct documentation for expenses. It is very important that you fill out the expense report correctly."

SOMETHING A LITTLE STRONGER

When we are disciplining subordinates, or, in our terms, trying to create more favorable behavior, an adult viewpoint is needed. If we state our position from an adult viewpoint, then the results become the employee's choice, not yours. It is important here to allow for a give and take in the conversation. Otherwise the conversation can become quite "parental" in form. Our goal is to communicate the importance of the issue. Our frame of reference here is to avoid phrases that come across as saying "do it this way because this is what I want." Our vocal tone is to be assertive, not aggressive. Our body posture is still open. These are still adults and we believe in adult-like treatment. This goes to the heart of Golden Rule treatment. We stop being seen as "mom" or "dad" on the job. We stop punishing them and begin treating them like adults. Adult-like treatment involves taking risks. It means shifting how we deal with people and this means changing ourselves as well. Change is uncomfortable whether it is for the employee or the supervisor. This change is going to ask you to look inward to yourself and to choose new patterns of one-to-one handling. If the first techniques we just looked at did not achieve the desired results, we must not revert to old aggressive habits. Instead, we look again to more positive and adult-like ways to deal with behaviors that are unsatisfactory.

> We stop being someone's "mom" and "dad" on the job. We stop punishing them and begin treating them like adults.

Various ways are available to become more assertive and yet not extend into an aggressive mode. Below are two techniques that have proven successful through years of use by a number of companies. The nice part of both is the retention of control by the employee. This is combined with keeping the supervisor out of an order-giving role. The techniques are

- "Play it again, Sam"
- "Lay it on the line."

These, as do many of the techniques, have peculiar names. In every case they have been named by people in the training programs. They found the odd names easier to remember and to recall what encompassed the technique. The basis for these approaches comes from the literature on behavioral psychology and has been adapted to the work setting.

"PLAY IT AGAIN, SAM"

The key to this way of dealing with people is persistence. You never let up. "Nag" may be another word for it. "Play it again, Sam" was the label given by the management group at JLG Industries, a large producer of mobile aerial work platforms and materials handling equipment. The technique is a combination of persistence and assertiveness to express an idea over and over again until the employee gives in to the idea. Certainly a direct order could be given and this would save time. However, in doing that we have reverted back to autocratic techniques that are less productive.

If the employee agrees, even half-heartedly just to shut up the supervisor, it still means it was her idea to change and not yours. The person remains in control of her life. Her dignity and self-esteem are kept intact. This is certainly in line with Golden Rule philosophy, and the philosophy is the key. If we have a firm grasp on the philosophy in the broad array of situations that confront us, then any technique that reinforces this will be successful.

That means you can make up your own lines, be creative—you know your work world better than anyone in terms of what might be successful. The example below is for illustrative purposes. Your supervisory responses will reflect your work culture and setting. Understanding the philosophy of persistance is the key.

Play It Again, Sam Example

Supervisor: Your production reports are showing some significant variances. We need to look at them to see what we can do.

Employee: My production is fine.

Supervisor: Well, there appears, at least on paper, to be a problem. We need to look at them.

Employee: I am not aware of any problems.

Supervisor: There are some problems and we need to examine the situation.

Employee: There is nothing wrong.

Supervisor: Look, I understand. You don't think there is anything wrong. But I must answer for these variances and I need you to sit down with me and examine these.

Employee: Well, if we must, let's do it.

"LAY IT ON THE LINE"

To "lay it on the line" means we are at a point where we must achieve a behavior change *now*. Our previous attempts have gone without success. To lay it on the line means we tell the person what will happen if this current behavior continues. This is not a threat. It is a promise.

The supervisor must be able to implement the promise and must then carry it out if the change does not occur.

Steps in the Lay It on the Line Approach

- Begin by reviewing the record of attempts to elicit change.
- Inform the person of the consequences of future continuation of the undesired behavior.
- Give a specific time table to allow change to occur. Use your judgment. Something simple like failure to wear ear plugs can be quick, something like poor product quality may take a little more time.
- Follow up to give the positive news if change occurred or to enforce the consequences.

The supervisor must check, if unsure, that he or she can, in fact, carry out the consequence. Then be sure to carry it out. Failure in either category will render this technique ineffective, hurt the credibility of the supervisor, and hinder future attempts at its use.

Employees are not children, but the following example expresses in the extreme what can happen if we fail to carry out the terms: A mother and father go shopping for groceries with grade-school-age children. The kids are taking packages off the shelf and creating a mild disturbance. The mother lays it on the line—do it again and you will be punished. It appears to be working. The kids behave momentarily. However, the kids remember past threats from mom and dad. They decide it is only a threat and begin a mild disturbance, heaving a cookie box. Mom screams another threat and the kids have won: Mom won't punish and dad just wants out of there. The remainder of the shopping trip is a disaster.

Again, we must caution you in the use of this technique not to become aggressive. Let the consequences of the employee's continued behavior enact the punishment. If you become aggressive, it is another variable in the mix. It can become a power struggle, which is not our goal. Our goal is to correct behaviors, not win power struggles.

By using this technique we are calmly and professionally talking ourselves out of the middle. We are making a sort of agreement with the employee. Part of the agreement is what will happen if they break it. The supervisor is back in the role of facilitator of human resources, back in the Golden Rule mode.

Lay It on the Line Example

Supervisor: We have spoken on three occasions about your failure to wear the company-required sports coat while on duty.

Do you recall those discussions and why the necessity for the dress code? (Give time for response.)

If this behavior continues you will receive a three-day suspension notice.

I will be checking with you on your next shift. Do you understand what I just said?

Employee: Yes, if I fail to wear the jacket on my next shift I will be suspended.

Supervisor: That is correct.

This chapter has offered several techniques that can be used by the manager going it alone, that is, without the whole organization changing its current practices. Certainly, it can be used if the entire organization becomes a Golden Rule model of action. Again, these are not the only techniques available. This is not a certified Golden Rule program. The idea of the techniques is to gain the feeling of Golden Rule actions.

These techniques reinforce the Golden Rule philosophy in another powerful way. By using the techniques that are assertive and taking into account employee respect, emotions, and feelings, we are changing. Changing our behavior to "living" the Golden Rule philosophy in our actions on the job. We go beyond slogans and posters and give a strong message to people that we believe in this. We use these types of behavior in our interpersonal actions with employees. By our actions, we reinforce respect, dignity, and adult-like treatment in our lives at work.

Chapter 6

REDESIGNING ORGANIZATIONS

Research into current economic conditions by a number of writers, including books such as *Megatrends*, predicts that change is going to be the dominant theme in our environment for some time to come. Strong world market competition, technological change, the radical changes in Eastern Europe and other former Communist countries all have a force; and change is that dominant force. In our own market we are looking at hostile takeovers, mergers, and foreign companies buying out American industries. Probably the one constant we can count on is change. In our organizations we must be able to handle change. To be ready for the dominant environment of change we need to be characterized by the following:

- Interpersonal dynamics are needed that make the organization compete successfully in the domestic and international markets. To be able to compete against Western Europe and the Eastern European nations that are entering into the world market we must change. I predict the Eastern European nations to be the new "far east" competition within the coming years.

- Organizations need to be able to adapt rapidly to market conditions and technology changes in order to survive.

- Employees are hired for their range of skills. We need to be able to put talents where the job needs to be done. Next, we must have employees assume the responsibility of producing the product and handling the customer's needs.

- Continuous quality improvement is needed from employees who are emotionally as well as physically involved in the process. Quality is not a fixed point or place where we stop improving. Regular quality improvement means quality changes are continuous in our products and involve all levels from top management to the workers in the productive process and service delivery levels.

Are the preceding points new information? No, others have been saying this. In 1989 consultant Michael Donovan presented a paper at an Association for Quality and Participation (AQP) conference in Kansas City, Missouri. He spoke of a similar grouping of requirements that our organizations must have in the future to survive. Years earlier Peter Drucker wrote a similar theme about what is needed for success in handling a constantly changing environment. If enough of us keep calling out, it will be heard and the transition will occur. On a more serious theme, if enough business failures occur because of resistance and the use of old methods of management, the transition will occur.

These points indicate a major group of changes that need to evolve. For example, the teamwork concept rules out, by definition, the traditional use of seniority, performance appraisal, and job bidding to name a few. Skill-based employee usage also calls to question traditional job categories and narrow job definitions.

> As managers we must let go of unnecessary work rules in order to move forward.

Investigation into our organizations indicates that workers really don't know what is expected of them. Where is our organization going? When we "open up," when we share costs and marketing information, not the ultra-confidential data, our workers respond as our allies.

In a later chapter we talk at length about creating the mission of the organization. Let's not confuse that issue here. This sharing and "letting go" of unnecessary rules is the current area of emphasis. Our typical organizations are highly structured places. Creativity is often lost in rules that make little sense. In many cases work rules are used to avoid judgment and experience. It appears at times that managers believe that uncertainty in the workplace can be removed and employee behavior corrected and made predictable by generating more and more work rules. Rigid work rules often appear to be a symptom of mistrust between supervisors and employees. It's no secret why unions tie up management in work rules; they feel management is not a group to be trusted. This has a more far reaching impact than we might believe. A highly restrictive rule about eating at our desks or inappropriate rules on dress code affect our overall view on the organization, job, work quality, and creative energy to handle our work.

In Franklin County, Pennsylvania, the local newspaper printed a story in 1990 about the county commissioners issuing restrictive work rules. It appears the commissioners feared rats and other rodents and bugs might invade their new building if people were free to eat at their desks. Certainly the spirit of the rule is understandable, but the restrictive, archaic nature could have caused very profound negative effects. This building is filled with county workers. Many are professionals in the social welfare field who are dedicated to the delivery of services to the poor, needy, and children among others. Their schedules are erratic, the snack at their desk may be the only lunch break they take. They may be granted more break time, but this group of people often works many hours without overtime pay because of a belief that what they do has social meaning. Their willingness to work for pay levels that are restrictive and put in long hours without overtime is part of their "gift" to society. Silly rules about work desk snacks can injure this spirit.

The quantity of rules, the "do nots," whether written or unwritten, rarely decrease unless we consciously decide to put our energy there.

I called on the Department of Corrections in a local state correctional institute and I asked them how many items are on the "do not do" list for prisoners. I took that number and quickly compared it with a few typical personnel manuals. It turns out to be fairly close on who has more restrictions: the average prisoner or the average worker! It's no wonder absenteeism is a problem in America. We are not quite sure if we are prisoners or workers. Absenteeism ranges from three percent, a figure considered good but still too high, to near twenty-five percent in the coal industry, to a whole host of other ranges considerably beyond two to three percent.

Many of our policies are negative in nature and geared to the two to five percent of the work force who cause the problems. In my experience ninety-five to ninety-eight percent of our employees are good and careful, but get a bad message from management. Let us turn the table around. We can write personnel policies for the ninety-five to ninety-eight percent who are good. Deal individually with the small percent. No matter what you do, there will always be a small percent who are difficult. Here are some examples of what I mean.

POLICY RESULTS

Some of the examples here are from H. B. Reese corporations, Certain Teed Products Corporation, Hagerstown, Maryland; Rohr Industries, Hagerstown, Maryland, plant, and Telecommunications Products Corporation, Chambersburg, Pennsylvania, among others. The following points are examples of what is possible:

- The concept of a paid attendance program. If you are sick, you are an adult, take off. You don't need a doctor's excuse to prove it. There is no set number of days you are allowed to be ill. You know what your job is and you are paid to come in to do your work. They want you there when you are healthy.

- If someone dies, you know how much time you need to handle the grieving. You don't have to prove any direct relationship. Some of the most cumbersome benefit policies and paragraphs I have ever read deal with bereavement issues. If it's a mother you get so many days, an uncle so many days less, and—heaven forbid—it might be the best friend you ever had in life and you cannot get off at all. This is not treating people with dignity and respect.

- If you need a personal day, a half day or whatever, take it. You are an adult. Work it out with your coworkers. The employee and coworkers know what has to be done in order to produce the product.

- The employees on the line hire and train the workers with strong positive results. Employees help bid for new company orders. Yes, that's correct, the employees are so involved in the job that they help produce the bids for the new orders.

With Golden Rule Management, we don't want first-line supervisors to be running around punishing people or waiting for mistakes. We want to hire all people for their skills. Our goal is not to hire into jobs with narrow descriptions. People are hired because of skills that will allow them to work or expand beyond any narrow job description. "It's not my job" is a message rarely heard anymore.

Results of Adult-Like Treatment

- Sick leave usage down significantly, and this is with no upper limit on its use. No, we aren't creating mini vacations.

- Bereavement usage down.

- Personal day usage down and not disruptive to the production process even among those companies doing assembly-line tasks.

- Absenteeism down significantly below the two percent rate.

- Turnover is rare on the job.

- On-the-job training time cut in half.

- Quality levels of products setting new highs.

DO UNIONS CREATE PROBLEMS?

I hear people say, "I have a union, therefore I can't be this creative, I'm locked in by my labor contract."

"Unions are only dragons in the minds of managers."

Rohr Industries has the United Auto Workers, Certain Teed has the Steel Workers, Hershey has the Bakers and Confectioners, none of which are pushover unions. Yet, all are operating in various avenues of trust and respect with teamwork and new concept ideas of management. In talking with the human resource manager at Rohr Industries, the traditional old labor contract went from almost a thousand pages to a nontraditional contract that is forty-four pages long. They went from 537 job classifications to five charter statements of work. Seniority changed from department to plant-wide seniority and forty-five work rules went down to one: counseling (we'll explain this more later). Sick days went from a set number to a paid attendance policy. The bells, clocks, and buzzers were removed. Reserved parking was eliminated. Special clubs for the salaried people were eliminated. Vacations can now be taken in four- or eight-hour increments. Guarded controlled access has been eliminated. Cost of living increases have been changed to results-sharing increases. Grievance procedures have been changed to problem-resolution procedures. Unions are now involved in decision-making. The titles of supervisors and union representatives have been changed to leader. The union contract went from a three-year to a five-year agreement. Most important, the traditional decision-making framework of upper management deciding and then passing it down through the hierarchy has been changed to one that more successfully gains a commitment from the employees, to a decision-making system of empowerment and adult-like treatment. The human resource manager has since moved to another organization, but in our last conversation indicated that the same direction would be used with the new employer.

It is our own inability to relinquish unnecessary controls over the lives of other people that create our problems.

There is no doubt that unions have been exploited in the teamwork process. They have been tricked into supporting programs that are basically to please a "stock analyst" and result in no real changes. Many companies have created the "Team *Whatever*" title. The reality is there is no substance behind the public relations phrases. There is no sense of community in the organization, only a public relations or marketing program.

Dignity and self-esteem are not raised in programs dominated by supervisor and manager suggestions. The union movement has stood for worker autonomy. A program that does not enhance this should be opposed by workers, unionized or not. The idea of Golden Rule Management is to enhance worker autonomy through adult-like treatment. This is why it has succeeded in unionized settings. It fits nicely with union objectives and goals. It is how we all wish to be treated. Unions respond positively to respect, fairness, and honesty.

Unions are only dragons in our mind. It is our own inability as managers to relinquish all the unnecessary controls over the lives of other people that creates our problems.[6] To add strength to this argument the quote goes to the heart of the control issue. It goes so far as to imply that control is preferred over commitment.

> Managers hate surprises. . . . Ask a manager to choose between creativity and reliability in subordinates and without hesitation the answer is reliability. . . . Expectation and realization must match. The reward is a reputation for reliability. A manager may be moving in the wrong direction, but this fact is often obscured by the aura of reliability that surrounds a steady performer.
>
> To meet expectations, managers depend on controlling the behavior of subordinates. . . . The behavioral control arises from benign structures embedded in process. . . . It is more rewarding to do what is expected than to deviate from standards of behavior. People also cooperate because they have no alternatives readily at hand. The end result may be cooperation but not commitment! (Zaleznik 1989)

I know of a UAW local union president who wishes to enact Section 301 of the National Labor Law, which says, in essence, if the union fails to defend the worker properly the workers can sue them in court. This UAW local president now desires to handle this legal responsibility by counseling marginal workers, not by forcing issues or taking a questionable union member's complaint to arbitration. This process can waste both time and money for them and the company. However, the stumbling block is management. Managers who fear the gray areas of participation, teamwork, and joint decision-making block this productive solution. Our organizations

---

[6] The reader is referred to two good sources on this topic: Shneider (1991, pp. 169–190) and Kets de Vires and Miller (1987).

should not be shaped like pyramids, but perhaps circles inside circles or spheres that are fluid and change form with longevity.

Golden Rule Work Environment
- Where we manage our own behaviors as workers
- Decide our own vacations
- Hire people for their skills
- Continually expand employee skills
- Share the vision of the organization
- Share the results of the success equally
- Where there are virtually no managers, instead there are facilitators of organizational goals.

Golden Rule Management can be a vehicle to swing companies to a strong competitive model. Let's unleash the power of our workers as creative vehicles for productivity in our organizations. Organizations who have elected this participatory style have experienced significant increases in output. Some report increases as high as twenty-three percent. This is a situation in which the worker, the manager, and the organization all win!

TASK TEAM BARGAINING—THE NEW WAVE

Recently, at San Georgio Pasta Company, both a giant step forward in Golden Rule Management and something new in the field of human resource management took place. The idea was to settle the labor contract by problem-solving methods, not by labor versus management across a table. I had been writing and discussing the possibility of this technique for some time and with various companies.

This technique used a broad cross section of hourly workers, union, and management viewpoints. The mission was to create a document for the hourly workers—not for the union and not for management. The prime mission was for the worker. Few unions or managers can claim their contracts are really in the best interest of the employees, not when it takes nineteen years of education to understand the average labor agreement, not when the whole process is designed to be adversarial. How can that benefit the worker? To this point in time, little progress has been made in the techniques of reaching labor agreements. Aside from the introduction of some personal computers and software, the process has remained unchanged since the early 1800s.

Negotiated agreements that were to represent the interest of our workers often failed to reach this goal. At many companies the past contracts are looked on with some mistrust. Many workers felt special deals had been arranged. Yes, it appears they felt their own local union leadership followed their own personal agendas versus the needs of the workers at large. My experience as a consultant and professional negotiator indicates this is not a phenomenon peculiar to any one company. It is my experience that many organizations have labor contracts developed by the old archaic and unsatisfactory systems. Like many aspects of the union-management environment, negotiations evolved unplanned with little research to direct its path. Negotiations evolved to their current state from the early days of our union growth era. The traditional way of negotiation has remained intact because of the many national labor laws that reinforce our adversarial system. The move to Task Team Bargaining (TTB) is an exciting and dramatic departure.

The goal of TTB is to create a nontraditional agreement that encapsulates the essence of Golden Rule Management. The key points of respect, dignity, and adult-like treatment are to be included. The process reinforces the concept of worker autonomy, making it consistent with unionization. The process is filled with problems and is certainly not a quick fix. But the feeling of having some control over their own destiny is the rallying point of the workers. Members of the various task teams who have had traditional collective bargaining experience remark how much better this approach seems to be: better in the sense of having creative solutions to problems, better in the understanding of each other's problems, better on the decrease of tensions and stress associated with traditional negotiations. The union has its agenda and management has its own. The employees in this process feel a sense of presence and empowerment that has never been granted before. When the process breaks down to position taking, very quickly a "time-out" is called to get the parties refocused on the problem. To rest on positions returns us to old habits and we lose the creative edge.

SOME NUTS AND BOLTS OF TTB

The team members are selected from a sign-up sheet. That is, the topics to be discussed (each side's demands) are rewritten as problems to be solved and then posted. If a person has an interest in an area he or she signs up. The first person to sign up is the first selected. These individuals are then subject to group availability. The goal is a broad base of people participating.

The system of selection is not perfect. Some hard-core unionist and hard-core nonunionists might come on board. Yet, these extreme viewpoints add to the credibility of the results.

Snags exist in the handling of economic issues. Hard-core position taking often takes place. Trust is a major factor with economic issues. The future use of this will involve holding down debate and keeping to the problem-solving mode with economic issues. Despite these snags good results are achieved. For example, calls from a chief local steward and others in the work force at a company reinforced to me the success of the program. Never in my experience have workers pointed with pride to "their" input. They considered it theirs because they decided the final language. The chief steward at one company expressed her satisfaction in having a contract where the whole process was up for scrutiny by everyone. No post-contract discussions of deals were made.

During the entire process of TTB, I recommend minutes be posted for everyone to read. Yes, the veil of secrecy should be removed. Trust the workers. In the attempts to date, no one has leaked anything to the press. If a special-interest group took exception with the progress of a team it was handled at the next session, before the clause was agreed to and the process finished. This makes the group consensus process very smooth.

The veil of secrecy is removed with TTB. An environment of trust is created where everyone knows what is being said and no one has yet leaked information despite the bulletin board posting.

HOW TO ESTABLISH TTB

A key step is training. If we cannot understand how to problem solve peacefully, the process breaks down quickly and we revert to our old habits. A bonus to remember, the training for TTB adds to the skills of the work force and facilitates the overall team-building process. The discussions with union leaders and employee leaders is very important. Gaining union support is not mandatory but it certainly starts the process out on a more cooperative note.

Steps in Setting Up TTB

- Meet with union officials to discuss planned format changes to the process.

- Meet with employees and supervisors to inform them of what the planned changes mean to them.
- Train members in problem-solving techniques.
- Train the team in conflict management.
- Train in team-building methods.
- Rewrite demands so they are stated as problem-solving statements.
- Set up a schedule of meeting dates.

PROCESS USED IN TTB

Are these task teams without conflict? Are they a new fad or quick fix to complex labor problems? The answer is no to both questions. They are a viable alternative to foster a more productive long-term relationship. There are some key points to using TTB.

Key Points in TTB

- Use a consensus versus majority vote for decision-making.
- Brainstorm to ensure total participation.
- Choose groups of six to nine people for each task item (formerly called demands).
- Write all items on a flip chart or board.
- Use a neutral facilitator to lead the group.
- Always agree on the goal of the group in the beginning.
- Employ group problem-solving methods.

Consensus is new for most workers. Consensus means minority opinions are respected and encouraged. To agree means you can live with the majority idea, not that you have been outvoted. It takes some initial care to keep from just taking a quick vote and overriding the minority views. Brainstorming is easy to teach and use. Brainstorming is a process of going from person to person so everyone has a chance to speak. Plus, it keeps everyone involved. Not all people are assertive; thus brainstorming ensures their participation. Group size is kept manageable. If groups are too big, nothing gets done. The neutral facilitator is free of union or management politics and can keep the process on track. If trust is an issue, in the first attempt at TTB, the neutral facilitator being an outsider to the organization is a real plus. Everything should be on a board or flip chart to maintain a common language from which all can work, rather than dealing with the confusion of working from six to nine sets of individual participant notes and interpretations. Never assume everyone knows why you are there. Always agree on the purpose of the meeting. Gain consensus on what is to be accomplished. It is a major factor in keeping the group focused on outcomes. If we all agree upfront to the goal and expected outcome, then this type of error is reduced.

> The goal of TTB is to create a nontraditional agreement that encapsulates the essence of Golden Rule Management—respect, dignity, and adult-like treatment.

What if there were no union? Wouldn't that solve the issue? The answer is no. Many companies are managed along traditional lines and structures. While they are trying to change, they have many layers of management with rigid rules that are negatively reinforced. The past history of many companies is an autocratic managerial style. Task teams can be used to unravel difficult problems in employee relations where no union exists. The history and environment of many companies is adversarial, though both sides in many cases are moving toward progressive human resource programs. Task team bargaining can solve the issues where traditional adversarial position taking has failed.

Is there a storybook ending every time? Does everyone live happily ever after? The answer is no, but the story is not finished. The process is still "in progress" and TTB is an evolving concept. It takes time for new ideas to become adopted on a wide-scale basis.

Courage is needed to try this. The first companies and unions I worked with are brave indeed. The senior management is taking a risk, as is the union. Yet the rewards to management are great in terms of a committed work force. For the union the rewards will be great as a model of progressive leadership. This first attempt did not change the world, but great progress has been made, and I feel this will eventually prevail as the model for bargaining. Nationwide TTB fits well with total quality management and world class management concepts.

Both labor and management are keenly aware that flexibility and understanding are required of both sides in order to survive. Yet flexibility is gained in very modest amounts, almost too little, too late in some industries by traditional bargaining. Task Team Bargaining provides a forum for achieving the changes necessary without "strong-arming" each other or resorting to threats. The net result is a work force more committed to the changes because they recommended and wrote them in the problem-solving sessions.

Chapter 7

THE GOLDEN RULE STRUCTURE

Meeting the challenge of bringing an entire organization into Golden Rule Management means confronting the changes that we spoke of in the last chapter. In addition, it means that changing our organization's style and structure is a necessary step. Organizations at this point try different things. It is obvious from reading the literature and from hearing speeches and talking to people that organizations are not oblivious to the market situation. They are trying to meet the challenges of international competition plus deal with problems they face in their own workplace. We see them trying increased employee involvement, decreased employer involvement, bonuses, changing product flows, on-line production changes to assembly lines, new ideas to change quality, mergers, divestitures, and cutting layers of management. In an attempt to meet the many challenges, we have seen organizations adopt quality circles, one-minute management, total quality management (TQM), just-in-time management, world class management, and a number of similar concepts.

These changes mean there is a realization that something has to be altered in our organizations in order for them to be successful. Each of these changes has helped overall performance. A problem pointed out by several well-known consultants such as Michael Donovan and Tom Peters is that these ideas are not necessarily well put together into a total plan. Most organizations have looked at a single aspect of change and have put all of their energy into that one item. They may have looked only at quality circle programs, for example, and have left out the whole idea of looking at job analysis, job description, product changes, even compensation systems. In addition, what makes it most difficult is that these changes have been attempted within the framework of our traditional pyramid management structure. In an earlier chapter, we said that in the new environment many functions from job bidding to seniority would have to be altered. The organizational structure that got us into trouble in the first place will follow us into tomorrow. Our current organizational structure has a significant impact on performance. I first became interested in organizational structure and its impact on productivity almost a decade and a half ago. This prompted me as a doctoral student to conduct extensive research on coal mine structure and how different mining organizations were designed and what differences in output resulted.

The research uncovered significant differences in output and productivity based on the organizational structure, including differences based on how we design our jobs and operating units, give out information, and set up the chain of responsibilities between individuals. The coal organizations were excellent laboratories for this type of work. We could, in the same geographic area, have two essentially identical coal mines operating with similar types of coal mined and seam size and similar levels of output. Operating a coal mine is not just a simple hole in the ground. There may be a hundred million dollar or more investment in each mine. A significant capital investment is necessary for equipment, machinery, and manpower training in each facility along with many workers. Since the workers live in the same area, it helps keep socioeconomic conditions equal for comparison. Since companies are mining the same area, transportation to market and a number of other competitive factors are constant and we can in effect control many variables in order to obtain a true result, or as true as you can get.

In the course of the study in coal mining, it was discovered that decentralized organizations outperformed centralized operations. Decentralized means workers assume more responsibility for output, quality, and other job-related decisions. It means moving authority and responsibility down the hierarchy. The more decentralized a company is at the operating level, the better the results. This had profound effects in later years as team management came into use. With team management, decision-making is moved to employees doing the job. This in turn sets up an efficient transition to a more streamlined structure. Now, the work is being done more efficiently, versus the scenario where we simply slash layers of management and the work is distributed helter skelter—some up the hierarchy, some sideways, some down—frequently without any efficient design. Often, in this slashing, work doesn't get done, which can seriously affect our relationships with customers. Streamlining implies significant cost savings via a leaner organization, the kind we will need to compete with in Europe in the 1990s and beyond.

In similar fashion, companies are reporting that getting rid of the corporate "cost cutters" and "bean counters" has increased morale. Team concepts may be a more sound way to handle economic downturns than before. When *The Wall Street Journal* began reporting on team management results to handle a crisis, a cheer rang out across the land; perhaps a more human and sensible way was upon us. Team management crossed over into areas we never dreamed of and it was working. For example, a typical way to handle economic bad times is to use accounting "hatchet" techniques and begin cutting, without input from employees. Now we have teams involved and the hatchet may become a thing of the past.

The coal mining experiments in organizational structure produced a lot of early results that have been a part of the Golden Rule design. Decentralization and teamwork are but two. Others included consistent utilization of policy across departments and remote facility locations to enhance productivity and quality, and the loss of rigid job barriers to total skill utilization of people. It also showed the positive impact of training and career paths for employees.

OTHER STRUCTURAL DIMENSIONS

In the real-life work situations of the coal mining operations, the differences between organizations were looked at by holding corporate structure constant in one company and noting the different structure in the other and measuring the output differences. It was from those beginning investigations that I saw a trail of events that results in higher output caused by key structural changes. In the current hierarchical structure, organizations function around some rather basic principles that have been with us a long time.

Current Problems That Plague Our Organizations

- Inconsistent policy applications
- Training programs without a clear connection to goals
- A work force defined by positions and titles, not skills
- Failure to decentralize
- Allegiance to a department or division, rather than the whole company
- Organizational structures that cause departments to function at cross purposes
- Information systems based on the trickle down theory

Let's look at each of the preceding points in more detail to see where they are causing us problems. Furthermore, let's look at some ideas to solve these problems.

Inconsistent policy applications.   There is a point at which we can have too many policies, and a point at which we can have too loose an organization. But more damaging than that is to be inconsistent in handling the policies you have. If you have three retail outlets, of which two accept personal checks and one does not, this is an inconsistent policy. It will eventually confuse customers as well as employees.

In older organizations inconsistencies are not uncommon. Many new areas of business or production operations evolved. As they evolved, they created their own rules. Some are simple, such as leaving the job site at the quitting bell—or can one leave a minute or two early and be walking out the door at the bell. While it is a basic item, if it is inconsistent between departments it can cause confusion. Digging out these types of differences takes time and energy. Some are such that we don't even see them anymore we are so accustomed to them.

Training programs without a clear connection to goals.   Training programs that do not support organizational objectives, reinforce the philosophy of the organization, or teach the skills required on the job are faulty. Training problems seem to cause yet other troubles. The result is infrequent use of the skills by the employees. For example, this random policy makes it difficult for employees to see the fit of their training to the vision of the company when their training is complete.

A work force defined by positions and titles, not skills.   In this situation, narrow job specifications and many job classifications are used to handle the work in the organization. Attention is directed at the position, rather than on the skills and how employees can be used to help the whole organization. The result is workers who have a narrow focus and don't have a picture of the entire organization or the entire product. The focus is so narrow that in many organizations I've been in, individuals have never been to the other end of their own plant. How has this problem been overcome?

The solutions vary, but one that has worked well is to send factory people to the end-user to see for themselves how the product is used. In large integrated operations, this may result in sending employees to another part of the operation because they are, in effect, the customer. Several years ago Certain Teed Products sent vinyl siding plant workers to visit crews at home construction sites to learn firsthand about the product and gain a full picture of the product and how their job contributes to the success of it. Telecommunication Products Corporation (TPC) has employees visit user sites. Does this always work? No, I have been in situations where this technique has produced no changes because the employees saw no reason to change in spite of the visit. There was never any message conveyed that caused the worker to seek change individually or organizationally.[7] This tells us that we need to do our homework and be sure the message to be learned and the objective of the visit are clear.

Failure to decentralize.   A centralized workplace is a problem that hampers us competitively and an area we addressed earlier. Golden Rule concepts allow senior management to "loosen up" and decentralize power and authority.

Allegiance to a department or division, rather than the whole company.   In many places we act as if each department or division were a separate island. The result is a focus on this micro-level of efficiency versus doing what is necessary for the entire organization's performance. This is not to confuse separating different products to track results. What we refer to may involve having a marketing department, a sales department, an accounting department, a purchasing department, all of them often separate from the production or operating units of the organization. Similarly, it could be the fabricating division and the lighting division working as separate units. All of them feel that they are the most important to the organization's success and each may in fact establish policy or procedures that could negatively impact the product or service of the whole unit or company. When we have loyalty and commitment focused on our departments, then this same energy is absent or reduced for bigger objectives such as those that include our customers, product, or service quality. Strict departmentalization reduces the ability to have a vision that includes the entire organization.

The most common thing I hear when I walk into an organization is that sales is the kingpin, and without sales, nothing else matters. Sales, marketing, or advertising may be a focal point of an organization. Changes seem to vibrate out from them in order to make them efficient, at times reaching the point where the operating group that produces the product becomes inefficient and as a result the sales begin in due time to suffer, sort of like the tail wagging the dog. Does that mean the operating unit ought to vibrate the whole organization? No, the entire unit needs to operate as an efficient network. Vibrate at the same rate, if you will. At TPC, if they need to market a new software or hardware product, the sales team is increased

---

[7] For additional reading on this topic the reader is referred to Belasco (1991).

to give it the necessary push. It is not increased from outside the organization, but from within. People move fluidly where skills are needed. Are they as equally skilled as the primary sales team? Not in all cases, but to the extent their skills provide they participate. This can vary from helping to prepare a major mail campaign, to calling customers and informing them of the new product, to actually selling the new product.

Organizational structures that cause departments to function at cross purposes.   Organizations are often structured so that they separate staff, service, planning, and controlling from the production area. This means we have everybody involved in specialized staff groupings, which in effect may foster more loyalty to their profession than they do to the organization. It is critical that these types of departments interact, critical to the point of moving their offices next to the desks of the first-line production supervisors if necessary to drive home the point. It's the same negative effect when the art department is separate from sales who is in turn separate from marketing. They function at cross purposes and are unaware of each other's activities.

Our accountants become interested in accounting certifications and in developing their professionalism in accounting. Similarly, our financial managers are interested in certifications in their area of expertise. Our marketing people are certified. Even our quality circle people are worried about trying to figure out how to get certified so that their professionalism grows and their staff function becomes more powerful. Unfortunately, we often reward people based on this sort of accomplishment, on their individual goals, and fail to see whether or not they are, in effect, able to improve on the overall organization effectiveness. This doesn't mean doing away with certifications or continuing education. But why can't we cross train and rotate people through jobs to have a more multiskilled group? Why can't we base rewards on an overall organizational efficiency versus just our area or one person's certificate? Sounds risky? Sure, but the end result is a leaner organization of talented people able to move where they are needed and rewarded for overall success.

Information systems based on the trickle down theory.   Top management decides key issues and this information trickles down to those who actually produce the product. This results in a void at the worker level where the product is produced. We rarely share business information; for example, we don't even share with our employees where the key costs are in the product. Then we wonder why "they," our production, operating, or service people, don't identify with organizational goals and efforts. I've even had organizations tell me, "Well, this information will be too complex or too classified . . . too sensitive for the employees." We are not building, in most of our plants, the stuff that involves the security and defense of America!

Our people are also better educated than ever. We are "building" peanut butter candy, cereals, crackers, cranes, computers and a lot of other items that are not detrimental to anything. Where we have convinced organizations to share information, they have achieved dramatic results. Many companies have been pleasantly surprised to find that the more information they shared with workers, the more positive the response. Workers also accept more responsibility in handling the information and acting on it correctly. They didn't run and tell their competitors. They learned where the major costs were centered. They finally understood all the "fuss" from the accountants. It helped them focus concern for product success and company success.

> Our information systems are set up on the trickle down theory.
> Top management decides key issues and this trickles down to the
> worker. This results in a void at the worker level where the
> product or service is produced.

We too often integrate and organize based on the top people being the most important, with information filtering down in this way. We operatively set up our work groups into "tiny boxes," then put departments into "bigger boxes," divisions into yet "bigger boxes," and each box is not necessarily cut the same so that it fits nicely into an organized "bigger box." In the end we have a poorly made structure. The results are workers who are hired from the "neck down"—we aren't hiring their brains, we aren't hiring their loyalty, we aren't hiring their commitment. What we have are a lot of individuals trained to develop their own plans so that they are strong enough to leave our organization, or workers on our assembly lines who cannot wait to get home to do something "creative" with their lives.

This sort of patterning of our organizations results in a very rigid organization at a time in our history when what we need is highly versatile organizations that are able to react when necessary. What it results in is putting people into jobs and giving them a tiny narrow focus. They lose site of the overall aspect of the product and the overall goals of the organization. As a result, quality changes, often negatively, as quality control becomes someone else's job. Improvement of the product becomes someone else's responsibility and not our own. Meeting the demands of a highly

competitive market requires a committed work force, one that is able mentally to change and move according to the varying demands of the customer. Our traditional organizational structure may be a factor in putting a
ceiling on achieving the kind of dynamics we need. This first began to
reveal itself many years ago and is now more clear than ever—but there are
ways to survive.

THE SUPERVISOR AND THE WORKER ARE THE KEYS

The individual worker and the first-line supervisor are going to be the
keys to achieving the versatility we need in American industry. Therefore,
it is important for us to focus our efforts on redesigning our organizational
structure around these individuals instead of our top managers. As such it
becomes important to redesign our organizations around a "whole" job and
to increase the flexibility of those who do that job. That is, we must pick out
key work processes and put together teams of people who can carry out the
necessary actions with our supervisors as facilitators. Whether you prefer
to call it quality circles, joint labor management cooperatives teams, or
participative decision-making, something to that effect must come about.
There are certainly enough buzz words out there now from which to
choose. An apparent way to be a very successful consultant in America is
to discover a buzz word. We have had many theories and catch titles in
recent years and they lead people to rally around them. So if we can think
up a nice buzz word for this, it would help the process go quicker in
America. In one organization the management team could not agree on a
term or buzz word to use, because they feared it would be too Japanese, too
"new age," and so on. Finally, the chief executive asked them to consider
using no term. Just do it and forget the name. The management team liked
the idea and began the process.

The process of teaming, putting together a group to carry out the job,
gives individuals a better sense of becoming a business person. It also helps
them assume the adult-like responsibility for carrying out business goals
and objectives. As you can see, based on an earlier analogy, the hardware
is teamwork, the software process is Golden Rule Management. At TPC,
individuals were taught how to read profit and loss statements, balance
sheets, and other business data, how to understand what they were looking at, and how to get a feel for the sense of running a business. When a
team proposes a project at TPC, they even project bottom-line impact. Team
leaders have become facilitators of the process, not the gurus who decide
every aspect of the business or every person's work life. Anything that will
increase the network of skills and then integrate the operating workers into

semi-autonomous units is going to help our companies head in the direction of a work force that understands business goals and objectives and what it will take to achieve them. That is, we are moving from a pyramid-shaped organizational network into a group of interlocking circles that can change size and change their very makeup of participants as the needs change.

Very importantly, it means we as managers and supervisors have to change roles and not become the experts on our machinery or product as we did in the past. Rather, our goals change to become facilitators of the human resource component on the job. We have to see that our people become the experts. We have to see that workers have the tools, the training, and the support that build the product and get it to market. It does not matter if it is a service, an idea, or a piece of machinery. Next we have to integrate planning, control, and quality improvement, all within this self-contained team network so that it becomes a continuous process.

INFORMATION AND THE SUPERVISOR

The changes we are talking about involve taking another radical look at how we use information in our organizations. In most organizations, information is geared to be accessible to top management and understood by them and to be in a form that is primarily for their decision-making. Yet, they don't produce the product. They are not the organizational unit upon which success rides. We have our focus on the wrong end of the organization. Our informational system should be designed so the working team can use it and have it put in the most handy form for them and let it disseminate upward to top management so they "can" figure out what they need from these data. If we really believe the crucial element is the quality of the service and product produced, and at a cost that is viable in the marketplace, then this is not a hard concept to accept. We need to change our whole mode of thinking so this can happen, including how we structure our informational systems within the organization. In most organizations I visit, the information given to the workers on the line is in an unusable form. It is designed to be used by executives at divisional or upper levels in the structure and not for ready and easy use on the assembly line.

Finally, I have a suggestion to those organizations who have been getting the employees actively involved in quality circles, team building, joint participative management, quality of work life, or whatever term we use here. The suggestion offered is that we alter this slightly to be sure that the focus is kept on the team concept in the organizational structure and not on directing the activities toward an individual job or departmental focus only. To separate our activities into teams but reward and direct based on individual positions or narrow job titles reinforces the wrong behaviors. It sets in motion a process that sends the wrong message to employees, a confusing message. Am I a "team player" or still in my old job? This is a recurring theme; it means we have players who can fill in at most every spot on the team.

As you read, it begins to look like everything flows into everything else. Well, you are correct. There is a connectedness to everything in Golden Rule Management, an inability to draw clear lines between functions and responsibilities.

For many of us this has a familiar echo to our spiritual philosophy that also claims a connectedness among all things. If this message is coming through, then you are on the correct path. The path of Golden Rule Management speaks of balance and harmony between our work and personal life and the interrelationship among all aspects of our being. By achieving the balance and harmony, we improve both our work life and home life. In this situation, the worker, organization, and society all benefit.

Information should be designed for the work team and put in a handy form for them. Let it disseminate upward to top management to figure out what they need from the data.

THE STRUCTURE OF TOMORROW

I am regularly asked to draw a picture of the organization of tomorrow. Let me explain that it is dangerous to rely on pictures. A two-dimensional picture reflects my vision on this reality, yet it may not be the correct picture for the reality of a different person or a different company setting. Golden Rule Management is "software" for people within a structure. Therefore, any suggestions here are to show what will make this philosophy of handling people work better. Second, pictures are two-dimensional, but we are involved in multidimensional activities. People, with all their feelings and emotions, coupled with the dynamics of the organization become hard to depict in two-dimensional form.

The form envisioned is a circle, chosen for its continuous form. This circle will enclose other interlocking circles. Within the interlocking circles are networks of fishbone diagrams that give the schematic on tasks involved. There is no listing by jobs, titles, or traditional areas. Certainly people have principal responsibilities as their skills dictate, but the emphasis is on what the task dictates, and our skills are fitted to this form.

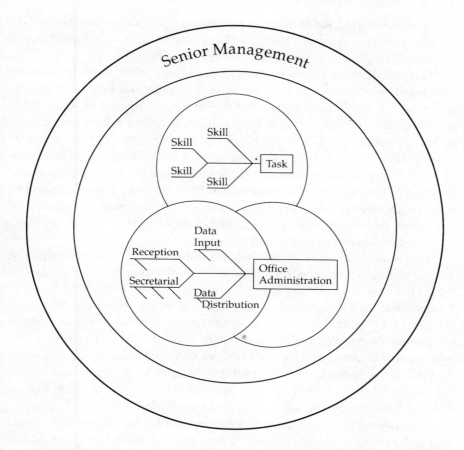

Each circle contains a group of closely related functions called *tasks*. These tasks can be products produced or services. Under each task are listed the members of the work unit as skills that are necessary for success. This includes supervision as a facilitative skill. The same person may appear on various diagrams depending on the number of tasks he or she is assigned. One task team may see the person as a secretary and another diagram may see the same person as the task leader. Remember the Frehn Center example where this phenomenon is common.

The interlocking circles indicate the interconnectedness of all our actions to the common mission of the organization. The circles and the fishbones are all fluid. The tasks change, the members change. Senior management is on the rim of the large circle. Every circle touches as if it rotates. This indicates the versatility of the service staff in facilitating the tasks to be accomplished. Another user of the Golden Rule concept envisions the form similar to a Rubiks-type cube, a popular toy developed by mathematician Erno Rubik with an infinite number of color solutions. The Golden Rule concept gives the user the ability to have an almost infinite variety of combinations of solutions as the need fits.

Has this drawing ever been used? Not in this generic form. It has been attempted over the years. It has been refined by organizations. Each organization where it was used found that it is at best an illustrator of the fluid nature of the company, not a fixed structure within which we change people as slots open. These organizations realized it was not necessary to have a picture fixed in time as the basis from which to work. Many years ago AT&T put out books with tiny little pictures of people in boxes above their titles. The book contained the hierarchy of the firm. Few of us want to return to those days. Yet many of our managers feel lost when we take away a structure and do not replace it with something else. The "something else" is what the individuals need from the organization.

This is no small point. In the early experiments it was assumed that the joy of a fluid job would be the replacement. In the long run, this is true, as it is in the case of a new hire into the system, who can easily step into this process. But for existing staff, it was different in the short run. When we removed their formal title and position there was a sense of loss and sense of identity crises. We quickly learned to hold hands and reinforce the whole-process nature of their work life, which proved successful. The same idea is basic to habit control. For example, if we have someone stop smoking, we must (in the short run) replace the habit with something else in order to have the person successfully quit smoking.

In whatever form Golden Rule Management is used, it can add a great deal to the organization. It can mean a lean, fluid, and efficient organization that will survive and be successful.

Chapter 8

PERFORMANCE APPRAISAL: ANOTHER GOLDEN RULE SECRET

As in all aspects of handling employees, the Golden Rule basics apply—treat people with respect, dignity, and in the manner in which you would like to be treated. In no other area of human interaction is this more serious. Performance appraisal by this system takes more time, effort, and energy, but the results are worth it.

Our top executives are paid large bonuses and stock options, even when times are bad and company performance is just average. One need look no further for proof of this than our auto industry where executives receive large bonuses while they turn in a lackluster managerial performance. Yet, at the very same time, the hourly workers are subject to wage rollbacks, benefit rollbacks, and deferral of pay increases. Our system of measuring and handling performance is so poor that the appraisal system seems negative or punitive in nature. This is exactly the opposite of what we wish. The following system offers some simple solutions to this problem.

For some time I had been consulting with organizations and trying all sorts of appraisal systems. More than a year was spent with a division of a major chemical company working on revamping job descriptions. The long-range goal was to correlate a plan whereby the job description would also be tied to the performance appraisal system, which would in turn be tied into pay. The long-range plan was to achieve "criterion-related validity" in the process. Criterion-related validity sounds impressive, but all it means is that each part of the system does what it says it will the vast majority of the time. For example, you are actually being rewarded and paid for what you were hired to do. Yet, despite the many hours of work and the mathematical criterion-related validity, the results were not achieving the expectations. Unfortunately, I was never able to try with them the system you are going to learn. In fact, it was after this experience that this performance process came about.

It was by chance I came across Marion Kellogg's book, *What to Do About Performance Appraisal* (1975). The book was not technical in nature. It stressed the interpersonal, one-on-one aspect of appraisal. It was like a light bulb turned on in my mind. I was pushing so hard to find a technical solution to appraisal, one that would numerically quantify and justify performance that I had overlooked the people aspect. For all my preaching and talking, I was not practicing my own stuff. I was not using Golden Rule concepts in performance appraisal. It began as a process of experimenting with the concepts on a person-to-person basis and paying less attention to the technical appraisal system used. The results were dramatic to me. Let me give you some examples. From banks to high-tech concerns, people were experiencing the changes and results they had dreamed of.

> Supervisors can use this process without any new investment, or for that matter, without the boss even knowing what they are doing.

It turns out that most of us felt the need for a technical system to hide behind. Most of us do not feel competent in handling appraisal. There is a presumption that those who appraise are able to coach and correct employee performance. This may or may not be the case depending on the level of training supervisors have received. This system relaxes the fear and puts in its place a process to achieve results you can understand and use. Also, a good point for first-line supervisors, you can use it with no disruption of your current system. That's right, you can use this without your boss having to invest big dollars in a new system. For that matter, the boss does not have to know what you are doing.

> Performance appraisal used well is the secret of top performance supervisors.

CONTINUOUS IMPROVEMENT AND APPRAISAL

Use of this technique will establish the basis for achieving continuous improvement. It is the idea of continuous improvement that is the key to many Japanese and German management techniques. This means we can take this unpopular task of management to the most important level of our job. With the changes it will be a task to which both the supervisor and employees will look forward.

Everyone can reach positive levels of competence, but we must believe these results to be obtainable. We must remember that our role is not that of task master looking for mistakes, but of a facilitator of quality and growth.

Continuous improvement and appraisal means that it is not a once a year task. The idea that we are facilitators of human resource development under Golden Rule concepts means we continuously seek ways to help people improve. A common complaint among workers is not knowing where they stand in terms of job performance. Are they doing the job well? Could they be better? Respect and dignity means that people have a right to know how they are performing. When we teach a person a new language, we help them with each attempt to pronounce the words in the new language. The language teacher does not wait until the end of class to critique the student. With constant attention during the class period, continuous progress can be made by the student to learn the words in a new language. The same idea applies here. If we want continuous improvement, our behaviors as supervisors, leaders, and facilitators must change. It must change from the periodic review mentality to one of regularly given direction.

Performance appraisal is the secret of top performance managers. Those that use it will achieve high levels of progress. Ignore it and you will end up asking why all the problems happen to you.

A DOWN SIDE TO THE PROCESS

What is the issue we are talking about? Is the current way of handling appraisal really that bad? Can it be such a major factor in limiting the performance of an organization? Douglas McGregor phrased the down side of appraisal this way:

> The conventional approach, unless handled with consummate skill and delicacy, constitutes something dangerously close to a violation of the integrity of the personality, managers are uncomfortable when they are put in the position of "playing God." The respect we hold for the inherent value of the individual leaves us distressed when we must take responsibility for judging the personal worth of a fellow man. Yet the conventional approach to performance appraisal forces us not only to make such judgements and to see them acted upon, but also to communicate them to those we have judged. Small wonder we resist! (McGregor 1957)

Social scientists like Rensis Likert are concerned about its impact on both employees and managers:

> The fundamental flaw in current review procedures is that they compel the superior to behave in a threatening, rejecting, and ego-deflating manner

with a sizable proportion of this staff. This pattern of relationship between the superior and the subordinate not only affects the subordinate but also seriously impairs the capacity of the superior to function effectively. (Likert 1959)

Before we go into a discussion of appraisal, a few issues of importance have surfaced over the years in my work with regard to appraisal. It is important to remember this goes to the heart of employee emotional "buy-in" to our organization. Treated properly, employees will gain a positive level of commitment to the goals and mission of the organization. This intrinsic motivation is essential for the type of success we wish to encourage. Positive levels of respect and dignity are essential here. The following is a checklist of items that, when followed, helps ensure positive results. While seeming to be obvious in nature, when ignored these items can lead to bad feelings and disillusionment.

Checklist for Appraisal

1. Why are you giving an appraisal? Is it a salary review, career planning review, probationary review, or performance review? Know the reason.

2. Use only job-relevant information. To do otherwise is a farce and should not be attempted.

3. Open the review process to input from the employee. Even the most "scientific" system has opinion as its base. Nothing is purely by the numbers.

4. Make sure your written and verbal appraisals are the same. Whatever you tell someone, be sure to write the same thing.

5. Have appraisal results open only to people who have a good reason to read them. This is a person's personal life. Common decency demands this respect.

6. If you are asked your opinion about a worker, and no appraisal has been recently made, don't talk about the person as if you had recently reviewed his or her performance.

7. Don't use another supervisor's appraisal without knowing the basis for it. That is, ask, how, why, etc., did the other supervisor arrive at this opinion. Their ideas of excellence may be different from yours.

8. Encourage a policy for how long you keep appraisals and stick to it. Make written appraisals available to all employees. Let them review their own.

9. Encourage policies so that all employees have the right to appeal the process.

This approach will take a different path than the traditional one with which we're familiar. It will change the very basic aspects of the process. First, do not emphasize the structure or form you use. That is, what actual document is used becomes secondary to the process. This is difficult for some people to accept because a lot of money was paid to a consultant who may believe the key to success is the form and structure. Well, the chances are that the form is fine if it is both reliable and valid (meaning it does what it says it will a good majority of the time). I am not suggesting you stop using the form and the consultant who sold it to you; chances are they are both fine. The typical problem is in how it is used. This process is going to ask you not to do the performance review, salary review, and everything else in one giant interview, once or twice a year. The Golden Rule performance process implies a different order of events.

KEY TO THE SYSTEM

The key to this system is in separating the process into its prime components and focusing our energy on each section individually. The key components are as follows:

- Career counseling review
- Coaching review
- Performance review
- Salary review
- Probationary review.

The idea is to treat each area individually and review each one at different times. The separation of the salary review from the performance review is critical. Both the reviewer and employee have separate psychological views for each, meaning that I approach a session talking about "how well I do my job" differently than "how much money" you're going to grant me on my raise. When we combine them in one setting, the probability is that employees will ignore the message about performance and listen for the dollar raise figure. Yet the goal of enhanced performance is very important and a prime purpose of the appraisal process.

A word to supervisors. When you first begin this process, don't be alarmed by employees being confused. Explain the process and why it's being used. But you still need to be aware that they will react in almost retreat behavior until they are sure this is for real and will last and is not a one-shot fad. At one organization where we have attempted this process, supervisors have slipped back to old habits to save time and conduct the entire process in one giant interview. Then, the next time they go back to separate sessions they face resistance. This back and forth action results in the workers never believing the change is "for real."

> The key to the system is in separating the process of review into its prime components and focusing our energy on each section individually.

CAREER COUNSELING REVIEW

The same message is true when we talk about a person's career and future goals with the organization. If we combine these items with salary review, we will lose the impact of one. Yet, we need to emphasize both. An employee's career progression with your organization is very important, and deserves special emphasis. There is a large body of literature that suggests there is a significant difference in productivity when organizations spend time and energy on employee career development. This means production and operating employees, not just white collar employees and management.

If employees do not have a vision of their possible progress with the company, they lose the edge. The career counseling review is scheduled as necessary; for instance, by semester to help night students select appropriate courses, semiannually for others to discuss seminars or career thoughts, or perhaps monthly for new hires. Remember, people like to talk about themselves and career talks foster commitment. Listed here is a seven-step program for handling the career counseling session.

Career Counseling Steps

1. The manager explains the reason for the discussion. This should only be a sentence or two.

2. The employee looks at their career to this point with us.

3. The employee expresses future career interests.

4. Offer comments about the employee's skills for these interests. Be sure to explain that your statements are only your opinion.

5. Then describe business needs for the future.

6. Offer career choices and implications.

7. Both agree on action plans and ways to achieve the goals.

Remember not everyone wants to be president. But we can still help achieve career actualization in the job area by further training, conference attendance, cross training, continuing education, and coaching.

Points two and three above are important issues for us. They imply that the employee will begin talking first. We want our employees to begin talking and express their interest freely, irrespective of business need or current incumbents. The motivational benefit of a person working toward a goal is the key to increased productivity. If we begin to talk before the employee, it will bias the outcome and resulting discussion. There is a sizable body of research that strongly supports career paths and career counseling as a way to increase organization productivity. Career counseling is not the same as career paths. Career paths are defined progression of advancement in the organization. Thus the process is an essential part of career counseling and extends it beyond our own organization's boundaries.

Limiting employees to discussing work life goals in terms of near-term business requirements has limited motivational potential. You shouldn't even limit their career goals to the organization. Remember, at the Frehn Center, career goals can be anything. If the employee wants to dream beyond the boundaries of our organization, and we can help them succeed, the organization will benefit by the enhanced productivity of an excited worker. The reality of many years of use of this process shows that many never go after lofty dreams, but for some the dream is what keeps them excited and committed to the job. At the Frehn Center we lose people who have achieved the lofty dreams. The positive effect on attitude and output this has on the ones who remain can be measured. Plus, it's the right thing to do. It's the Golden Rule in action, treating others the way you want to be treated.

COACHING REVIEW

Coaching comes to the meat of performance appraisal. In coaching we focus on one item or area of needed improvement at a time. We work with the employee and establish guidelines and time frames for improvement.

We follow up in short time spans to see if changes have occurred within the agreed guidelines. These meetings add to the level of information for judging the overall growth and development of the employee. Coaching is like a constant flow of positive reinforcement for desired changes. We know the fastest way to learn a task is by regular reinforcement of successful acts. That is why it's called coaching. The athletic coach doesn't wait until the end of the season to tell the players how they can improve! Well, neither should a supervisor. Coaching adds structure and form to the process. We could go on at great length about the positive psychological aspects of regular feedback. The "short version" tells us this stream of feedback produces a rapid learning curve. Our view is that people want to do a good job and coaching reinforces the good points and adjusts those aspects not on target very rapidly. The results have proven to be very positive. Again, individual supervisors do not need the organization to change to do this; they can start this on their own. Some helpful ideas are given next for handling a coaching discussion.

Coaching Appraisal Steps

1. Review information about the person's ability to do the job.
2. Review actual events concerning the employee's performance. This may come from the following:
   - Memory
   - Notes on key aspects of a job, both good and bad
   - Prior coaching evaluation forms
   - Other reports (salary, probationary, progressive disciplinary, etc.)
   - Employee self-appraisal
   - Notes of former managers
   - Personnel records.
3. Pick the area for change that will most likely result in better work. Describe what you will do to help.
4. Set a time frame to meet again officially.

PERFORMANCE REVIEW

The periodic performance review is a new experience with this approach. It now becomes a more global exercise that includes the following:

- Coaching reviews
- Career counseling reviews
- Probationary reviews (if appropriate).

Under typical systems, this annual event was the crux of the process. An unfortunate event is the pain of finding out we were doing our job incorrectly or not up to our bosses' expectations for the past eleven months. This actually happened to me years ago in my career. I was amazed that my boss allowed me to continue incorrectly for so many months. It turns out I was not alone. People have offered me dozens of tales of similar occurrences. The same confused feelings of bewilderment came over them as they did me.

This approach involves many sources of data and lets us see the improvement of employees in the coaching areas and how progress is being made to achieve career goals. Two checklists follow that are designed to help you follow through for a successful experience.

Steps in a Performance Appraisal Review

1. Know the career goals of the employee and if they are sticking to them.
2. Pick out the appropriate long- and short-term organizational needs that match the employees areas and the time table for such needs.
3. Figure the rate of change of advancement and current employees in those jobs that the employee has chosen as career goals within the organization.

Steps in meeting with the employee:

1. Talk about his or her job and your vision of it.
2. Discuss performance results expected by both your boss and yourself. Compare these to what actually occurred. Allow for employee comments and viewpoints.
3. Talk about job standards and how they are used for success.
4. Determine if there any obstacles to the person's success. If so, are there ways to overcome them?
5. What is your part as the supervisor in helping to achieve their goals?
6. Offer appropriate personal experiences and job knowledge to keep the personal emotional bridge present.

Our mission is to develop successful people, not to find ways to explain a small raise or no promotion. Offer additional manpower, money, facilities, and equipment resources to help them meet their goals if possible. If you are able, offer incentives for successful performance. Explain sources of help and provide them as needed. Finally, identify organizational and system changes that are necessary for employee success. This is a more global process and does not occur with the frequency of the coaching review; that is, the coaching review can be very frequent for new employees or persons experiencing trouble, at least quarterly. This review can be semi-annual and still be effective.

SALARY REVIEW

Salary appraisal is the area employees "listened" for under the old system; performance review and other information went in one ear and out the other. The result was the typical twenty-day-maximum motivational incentive derived from a raise. That is, if the raise was one that suited us or was significant in terms of amount, productivity did rise for a while. Otherwise, the session produced a disgruntled worker. After a series of years under this system, it is little wonder that people appear uninspired about their chosen careers.

Our goal is to avoid this trap. We achieve this in part by separating the salary appraisal from the performance appraisal. We are not going to talk about how to establish a pay system with all the steps and reliability and validity coefficients. Most of us have pay systems in effect. Whether they are perfect or not, we can work with them better by using this technique. Your same appraisal form is used with this appraisal as before. Some tips follow on how to handle a salary appraisal. Remember, this appraisal is the last step in the process and has all the information from the other appraisals to help. The only item discussed is how much you can pay the person.

Steps in Handling a Salary Appraisal

1. Compare the person's performance to the standards of performance. For your own information, check their pay with that of other employees with lower ratings.
2. Review the past performance session.
3. Do not delay or apologize for the raise. Present the figure in a positive framework. If you are bound by policy, tell the person about the constraints, but don't apologize, you didn't write the policy.
4. Make good (not staring) eye contact.
5. Then, allow the person to talk, they may vent (tell) their feelings in a negative fashion. Don't debate here. Let them vent for awhile. Actively listen and respond positively about your feelings toward him or her as an employee.
6. Conclude the session on an upbeat note.

The session will necessitate your understanding of some basic facts, including the following:

Salary Information

1. Salary philosophy, plan, and practices
2. Amount and frequency of increases
3. Limiting business conditions
4. Job grade, if established
5. Minimum and maximum for the job, if existing
6. Specific ground rules for earning an increase
7. Employee's job responsibilities
8. Work results expected of the employee
9. Measures, criteria, standards, or ground rules for success
10. Market value of the person outside the company.

In some organizations this task is easy. Raises are set by law or the organization has lots of money to give. In financial organizations (banks, credit unions, etc.) and most service sector jobs, however, this is generally not the case. A salary review is very difficult when you cannot reward a top performer. The separation of the process truly helps. You are not telling them they are great with a followup of a small raise. You stick only to the small raise topic. This is called making the best of what you have.

PROBATIONARY REVIEW

The effective handling of employees during the probationary stage is crucial. During this time period we establish the behaviors and expectations of success. During this period an employee who does not work out successfully leaves without negative consequences. The active use of the coaching appraisal is the general rule. By active we mean concentrated supervision and short-term time frames for evaluating success. A few ground rules are listed next for successful handling. Many corporations, universities, government research units, etc., have longer probationary periods for their professionals. For example, the probationary period of a professor can be five years to achieve tenure. Because they are professional or because the time period is longer is not a reason to ignore the ground rules.

Ground Rules for the Probationary Appraisal

1. Move quickly to give the person a chance to improve.
2. Be honest about changes that are needed so that the employee understands what is expected.

3. Let the person raise and discuss job problems.

4. Have many short sessions (versus one long one) to cover appraisal, work problems, and goal setting for the probationary period. This gives time for adjustment on both sides.

5. The probationary period should terminate with respect for both of you.

6. Document more than normal during the probationary period. This gives adequate information for the final hiring decision.

CONCLUSION

This multistep approach takes more time to handle, but the road to continuous improvement in quality and service is not easy. Furthermore, the handling of the human resource component—the people—deserves this level of attention. When I coauthored a book on employee benefits we found that an organization will spend more than two million dollars during the career of the average supervisor. That is a lot of money. A two-million-dollar piece of machinery would receive a lot of tender loving care (TLC), regular maintenance, repairs, and the like. Certainly an employee deserves the same degree of TLC as a machine. The tie-in to respect, dignity, and adult-like treatment emerges as significant in the eyes of our workers. Using this multistep process shows there is no mistake that we are concerned about them and their performance from all vantage points.

Chapter 9

GOLDEN RULE PLANNING: TURNING THE PROCESS UPSIDE DOWN

The mission of the organization—the vision of our leaders—is a road map to where the organization is going. The Golden Rule path is the quest for quality, the quest for excellence, the quest for respect and dignity. The path to achieve new heights in all these areas must at some early point be described. Somewhere at some time you will have to put in writing, or articulate very well verbally from person to person, what you are hoping for and the purpose of the organization. Fail to do this and no amount of training or restructuring will help. The quest for excellence will always escape your grasp.

In many places this is called the "mission statement" or "statement of purpose" or some similar term. Many organizations have these written down and have them posted on walls in the hallways and walk areas. But that is not enough. In fact, most people in most organizations I go into could not even begin to tell you the mission of the organization. They know vaguely, for example, that they make candy, or they produce steel, or they sell cars or furniture, but that's it. They may know the general purpose of the organization and think that the whole mission is just this one aspect.

> Mission statements must be personalized to every individual in the organization.

Mission statements are often lofty-in-the-cloud ideas that are written by higher ups in the organization at comfortable resort settings. They may describe in broad strokes what the organization is about. This is okay, this is needed, consensus must be reached at the top levels. Unfortunately, that is where most organizational mission statements stop. Rarely do we find that the mission statement extends to every individual in the organization.

I don't mean copying the results and distributing them. I mean personalizing them. Most people, on hearing this statement, scratch their heads and say that could become a very complex process—and they're correct. A mission statement can be broad at the top management level, but as it goes down the hierarchy in an organization it must be continually refocused to each person at his or her appropriate job point, all of which takes time, energy, and planning. The refocusing of this is critical if we are to understand how each person's efforts directly contribute to the success of the organization. That is, how are my efforts, right now, going to contribute to the success of this organization in achieving what is written on that mission statement? This does not imply that we need separate missions statements for everybody or have a whole manual written on the mission. It does imply that we must take careful time and energy and have the mission statement in front of us and be able to write or articulate clearly to every person we are responsible for where they fit in this statement.

Many organizations take the effort and trouble to create what is called a strategic planning document. For some, the idea of strategic planning is what the mission statement is all about. That is, they go to great lengths to describe in terms of what is going to happen in the next six months, the next year, or the next five years where they want the organization to be and road maps to get to these points. In the organizations that do it more efficiently, the strategic planning process involves, in broad terms, information coming down from top management about their vision and plan of where they see the organization going. Feeding back up the hierarchy is the response about how to achieve these visions to get a two-way cross fertilization of ideas to achieve these goals. If done properly, this can be a very powerful tool for focusing the efforts of people. Unfortunately, this very powerful searching process often ends with a large document that sits on a shelf and is reviewed every so many years, and in time it becomes a process that is automatic. We update the figures, update the numbers, and put the same book back on the shelf. It loses the vitality of a "living" document. Many consultants have worked out new approaches for updating and reviewing such plans so that they are always living documents. The documents are kept alive by ensuring that employees are involved in the changes and know their roles. This serves to stimulate people on the job and make them feel as if they are a constant part of the success.

GOING IT ALONE

For our purposes, it doesn't matter if you call your meeting a strategic planning session or a mission statement session, but people need to know where they are and how precisely they are helping to achieve the goals.

Again, this doesn't mean the first-line supervisor has to change the organization. In fact, if you are going it alone on Golden Rule Management, you focus your efforts on your people and let them know what their part is in achieving success. Read this section with that attitude in mind.

I am one among many consultants and trainers for a number of organizations. An organization usually hires consultants for a specific topic, not to go organization wide with any one idea. In these circumstances Golden Rule Management is implemented in spots. That is, supervisors go it alone, not as part of a company-wide program. Frequently, this is how the program spreads to others in the organization. People outside the department watch the positive changes with interest and want to know more. Personalizing the mission statement for your employees is not a subversive act for which you will get into trouble. In fact, when your people are performing at high efficiency and attitude levels you may get promoted or receive some other form of recognition.

Remember, the Golden Rule concept is simply to treat others as you wish to be treated. We all wish to be included as to the direction of our organizations. It's our life's work, it feeds our families. It's the right thing to do. Employee apathy is a predictable outcome of years of "attitude" neglect by management. Let's help employees get back their enthusiasm for their life's work. A good place to start is the mission statement.

DON'T FORGET FEEDBACK

Fund-raising events have ways to show their progress. In sporting events the announcers regularly give the score or results of events. Yet, we often fail to tell people the score in reaching our goals.

Even some of the better strategic planning sessions and mission statement companies I've been with often fail in this key area. They fail to give regular feedback and follow-up to employees. They do not let workers know what steps have been taken to get there, what is working, what is not working. Rarely do we ask for their help or suggestions when times are tough. Congratulatory statements to the people on how their particular initiatives have helped achieve the company's mission are a rare occurrence. Yet, virtually all texts on communication encourage this.

How do we communicate this? We have to go back through the same process of up and down the organization chart to ensure that we have a follow-up network to get back to the individual. Yes, we must include the entry-level person in our organization, and be able to tell them thank you, because of your effective cleaning, or copying papers, or whatever, you have helped to facilitate this part of the mission of our organization. Every job is important. Every person is essential to success. If they are not critical or important, then that job can be eliminated or absorbed into some other aspect of someone else's job. The jobs may not be fun or exciting, they may be mundane, but if they are not critical they should not exist. People can be committed to mundane jobs if they understand where they fit into the success of the organization. The most frustrating comment I hear as a consultant is employees saying, "It doesn't matter what I do, the organization is going to go its merry way." There are very few things sadder in an organization than a statement to that effect. That means the person feels apart from the organization. It means the organization has not embodied its culture, values, and goals to that individual. We need to build bridges so that people will commit to the goals of our organization.

ADVERSITY OF GOALS

If our goals, mission, and culture are so adverse that people cannot buy into them, then we have to take a long hard look at ourselves. Many will lean back and say, "Well, obviously that is not a problem here." In these cases we should step back and take another hard look. If we have high employee turnover, labor problems, statements by employees that they can't "buy in," then perhaps we are creating an adverse atmosphere without even realizing it. For example, reserved parking spaces, special treatment for managers, special retirement accounts for executives, etc.—these actions create an adverse atmosphere for people with the result that they don't feel a desire to commit to the organization's goals and objectives.

When special projects are accomplished, do the managers stand up and take the bows? Is there a sincere thank you and a handshake for a job well done? Do they remember to invite the secretaries, who did all the work of putting the project together, to the recognition event? Recognition for clerical employees is a "ghost town" in U.S. companies. They are among the legions of unrecognized almost nonexistent people in our organizations. Supervisors going it alone do not need a formal system to say thank you. Nor do they need a formal system to give updates on company progress toward goals and where their people fit.

Success is being able to create the kind of atmosphere and environment that helps operating employees and supervisors buy into what we are hoping to achieve, to buy emotionally into Golden Rule Management. This may involve redoing our strategic planning, our mission statement, or whatever process. Yes, supervisors on their own can refocus the mission for their workers.

What about simultaneously starting the mission statement from the bottom up, instead of just counting on senior management to issue broad ideas? There is no rule anywhere that says the top manager has to be solely responsible for seeing the vision of an organization. In America we pay enormous salaries to executives to run our organizations and provide the vision, hoping that his or her vision connects properly with the buying public and the employees. The result of this gamble is that everything will be a "fine marriage." But that is a phenomenon that need not exist. We can capture the creative aspect of our employees and see what they feel our mission ought to be. Next we merge these values and attitudes with our top managers and judge to what extent we are all willing to commit to a compromised version of the goals. This can go a long way to help erase the problem of "the company going its merry way without me" attitude. Even mathematically it makes sense to include more people. The probability of "guessing" incorrectly is greatly reduced with the inclusion of more visions.

This process has been experimented with at TPC and Jerry Conn Associates, Inc. Both companies are under the parent company of American Visions, Inc. TPC is a high-tech system and software integration and design firm, while Jerry Conn Associates is a marketing and distribution company serving the cable TV industry. Teams of employees at each organization put together their vision of what the organization ought to be. The process produced some outstanding results and compromises from senior management. Was every idea a success? No, but the marriage of thoughts brought forth a commitment to goals and objectives that was not always present before.

CAPTURING THE VISION

A lot has been written about capturing the vision of the organization for all employees, from top management to entry level. I feel it is very important and have noticed in organizations that those employees who effectively capture and understand the vision of what the organization is, what it plans to do and plans to become, have a better grasp on what to do to help achieve that vision. In one of the more notable and famous ice cream companies in America they have even gone so far as to agree that a certain amount of profits will be donated to charitable works chosen in part by employees in an effort to help them capture the vision and their commitment.

Why is that important? If we can find several levels on which to gain commitment, whether it is the fact that profits are going to save trees or whatever, as well as the quality of our product, then we have employees committing on multiple levels. It is the same principle in banking. When a bank has customers who have a lock box, a checking account, a savings account, a mortgage, and a will-under-trust, it has commitment. That is, the more products or services customers buy, the more they commit to the bank, thereby reducing the probability the customer will leave as a client. It is the same type of comparison here; the more levels employees identify with, the more avenues of commitment we can gain and the higher the resultant probability of a committed person pursuing the quest for quality, excellence, and productivity.

Does this mean that we simply give a presentation to employees and then everybody buys into and understands what we are doing and all goes well, sort of like a thirty-minute situation comedy? Most of us realize this will not happen. Some organizations have had a history of extreme adversarial labor relations, of bottom-line thinking, or of never dealing with the people on anything but a surface relationship. In this case, going into mission statements, strategic planning, or vision sharing may be premature. We may have to back up and begin a publicity campaign, a bombardment of positive ideas that includes sharing where the organization should be. Doing this on a regular basis will set the stage for a program that will lead to pursuing these activities and eventually to commitment from employees.

Recently, this long process began with two companies: JLG Industries, manufacturer of platform lifts and cherry picker-type lifts, and Teledyne's Landis Machine Company. Both companies have a history of adhering to traditional organizational structures and following authority along a typical chain of command. Both companies are facing radically changing markets and competitors. At Landis many supervisors had fathers and grandfathers who worked there. Their frame of reference was passed down from dad, who got it from grandfather, and is well entrenched.

In these situations it is hard to move directly into vision sharing and strategic planning. Similarly they cannot jump directly into semi-autonomous work groups. The process of empowerment has to be handled one idea at a time. Fortunately, both organizations have top managers who are active and supportive. The new president of JLG is a Deming fan.[8] There are many links between the Golden Rule concept and how it fits with the Deming approach. The president's attendance at sessions and continued

---

[8] The reader is referred to the works of W. Edwards Deming. Dr. Deming is the person largely responsible for the success of the quality movement in Japan. He is famous for his 14 points of management as they relate to quality.

pushing for the management philosophy changes are needed energies to ensure progress.

Why is this so hard? For managers commitment seems to be easier to achieve. There are so many ways we can gain commitment as managers. Many avenues of creative expression are open to the typical manager versus our nonmanager group. If nothing else, the nature of education grants mobility, which allows for more flexibility. However, for the technical and blue collar, clerical, and entry-level people, these options may not be readily available. Their jobs typically are more directly laid out, which in itself may be poor structuring, but not everything can be changed immediately in an organization. We must pursue with energy and conviction ways to help the employees gain this level of creativity on the job. This will lead to the commitment, which completes our quest for quality and excellence.

HOW TO IMPLEMENT GOLDEN RULE PLANNING

Many fine books describe the planning process, so there is no purpose in reproducing that experience here. Our objective is to take the document and make it part of everyone's life on the job.

Steps to Implement Golden Rule Planning

1. Create a mission statement/planning document. In a one-to-one conversation break this wording down to recognizable goals with which the person can identify.
2. Use the job description of the person with whom you are speaking. This ties what they do to the mission objectives.
3. The annual report may be helpful to better visualize how the product is used and customers are served. It can reinforce the idea of internal customers, that is, the next person in the process concept.
4. Create key news articles that convey the image of the product and company. This is of particular importance if you are trying to change the public view of your product or service.

The ultimate action involves the actual encounter with the worker. You should have a reasonably private place where a conversation can occur and, if possible, it should be one on one. The key is to make the tie-in to the person and the mission. It's better to use small groups than to give up and not try because the one-on-one situation is impossible.

How to Capture the Vision with Employees

• Do not make the meeting seem like a burden to either of you. Keep it light, fun, and relaxed.

- Do not use this time to criticize performance. Keep the tone positive and about the tie-in to the mission statement.
- Use the following sequence as a rule-of-thumb:
  1. Briefly tell the person why you are together.
  2. Ask them if they are aware of an organization mission statement.
  3. Go over the statement.
  4. Spread out the job description, mission statement, and other brochures.
  5. Ask if they see any tie-in to them.
  6. Help them with the tie-ins to their job.
  7. Show the continuity from their job to mission statement to customers. Customers can be both the final purchaser or the internal customer they supply their work to in the organization.
  8. Allow feedback and ideas to flow.
  9. Schedule a follow-up later in the year to tell them how the mission is progressing.
  10. End the sessions on a light and positive note.

Supervisors who use mission tie-in programs find the process becomes a welcome occurrence by employees. It becomes a pipeline of positive information about the organization and their part in its success. It can become a platform on which to enact changes in behavior and attitudes, and it can be done without any fuss. That is, those supervisors going it alone can do this without a formal company policy. It is just good management or facilitation to do this.

THE TIE TO DIGNITY

How does planning tie in to respect and dignity for the employee? The plans so far indicate we are working very hard to make individuals feel they are an integral part of the success of our organization because of their contribution, that achieving their own knowledge of the vision of the organization is important. By this effort they have contributed to strategic planning because they understand the mission and how aspects of their job tie in to the organization's success. They are no longer mere employees doing a job, indifferent to the customer. Respect and dignity go hand in hand. It is no longer an "I'm your parent situation" or dealing with a paternalistic-type manager or an autocratic manager barking orders at employees, expecting them to act like robots or automatons just merely doing a job.

Under the Golden Rule concept, respect and dignity emerge through visions shared because "I want," as an employee, to make my contribution. "I" understand where my contribution will take the organization, and "I want" to be a part of the success. A big anchoring point for those of us in Golden Rule Management is to work very hard on the mission statement and vision sharing. Try to make this step the earliest point possible in the process, with a commitment to always go forward in vision sharing with your employees. Try to make it a regular event in your managerial efforts, not a one-time or special event.

But going forward in this area implies a decrease of managerial control. As with all aspects of Golden Rule Management, it implies reduced managerial authority and control over people. It means giving up to the individual some of the unnecessary control we had over their lives and letting them take back control over their own destinies. It implies a step forward for them, maybe several steps forward. For supervisors it is a giant step forward because it frees them of being responsible for this person's life and his or her thinking and success. (Although, the supervisor never really held responsibility for the employee, only the illusion of responsibility.) Ultimately, when our employees look back on their lives they should have a positive reflection. Our supervisors and executives should not be burdened with the thought of wasted or frustrated employee lives. Facilitating employee growth, development, and commitment to the organization is necessary.

Chapter 10

GOLDEN RULE SECRETS: TRAINING AND CAREER PATHS

TRAINING

One of the best descriptions about training refers to it as an art form. Many avenues and techniques are available to aid training, Ph.D.-level university curricula are devoted to it. Training is with us from the elementary school level through the doctoral level, the blue collar level, and the technical level. But training goes to the heart and soul of a lot of problems in American industry. Training must be an ongoing concern of every organization. It is no secret, and it has been well documented in many journals, that America lags significantly behind in the training area. The Japanese, the Germans, and others outpace us in time spent per person with training. Not all American companies have lagged in this area. Corning has taken tremendous strides in the last year to increase training. H. B. Reese Company, Hershey Chocolate, and JLG Industries are a few companies with which I am familiar that have worked on their training programs. Others, such as IBM, Xerox, and Federal Express, have made major money and time commitments to training. A number of smaller high-tech organizations across the country are striving to enhance their training capabilities. They realize that the benefits are significant. Training also has an effect in terms of cross training of people. Cross training means that we don't just train employees for their particular job skill; instead, we give people the opportunity and the privilege of being able to move to other jobs to learn new skills and get another look at how the organization is run.

Certainly, in times past, unions rejected this type of flexibility in the work force—and for good reason. If not handled with respect and dignity, flexibility was a way to exploit workers. However, the economic environment has changed and, in many cases, so has the negative aspect of flexibility.

A lot of jobs exist that aren't too exciting. We can get burned out or mentally tired of ordering the same supplies for the same products and arguing with the same suppliers every day, year in, year out. It serves as a great mental lift to do something different for a while and cross training can provide this tremendous mental lift. In addition, there are a number of rather obvious benefits to cross training that have been well documented in the journals. One is people being able to fill in when needed and to provide a base for future expansion of the organization. We are not going to spend our time here examining those points in detail because they have been well discussed.[9]

If you are on the fence trying to decide if cross training is worthwhile, we want to push you over the edge with some data that suggest it is not only worthwhile, it is imperative. Exciting latent benefits result from training and cross training, benefits that can add to the base of self-esteem and respect and dignity of our workers. How does that happen? The latent benefit is the enhanced self-esteem that an employee feels from the cross-training effort. They realize they are more valuable to the organization with the new skills they know, which enhances self-esteem. A number of psychology articles have tagged enhanced self-esteem to enhanced product quality and productivity. Both are objectives we must have for our organizations to succeed and both are stated objectives of Golden Rule Management. Another latent benefit is the positive effect this enhanced self-esteem has on the home life of our employees. A balanced employee is another objective of Golden Rule Management.

TRAINING IDEAS

Training for nontraditional students varies from the traditional pattern we experienced in our school days. Trainers must be more creative in capturing the imaginations of the learner. For many, it has been years since they have spent time in a classroom and the endurance to sit and listen has eroded with the years.

Tips for Training

- Keep everyone mentally moving in class. Any lecture should break at around twenty to thirty minutes. Then move to something where the

---

[9] For an expanded discussion on this topic the reader is directed to DeCenzo and Robbins (1988, pp. 240–263) and VanDyk, Nel, and VanZloedolff (1992, pp. 263–276).

participants are actively involved based on the lecture information. Also, have lecture material in other formats, such as print or audio or videotapes, so that participants have a choice of delivery methods.

- Use a multiple-receptor approach, that is, one that enhances learning in many ways with different senses. Use films, flip charts, lectures, case studies, and games as part of the total package.
- Try to arrange hands-on exercises. Adults learn best by doing.
- Use humor, it reduces excess stress, which can inhibit learning.
- Courses should have continuity. There should be an overlap from one course to the next in order to create the effect of relevance and how everything links together. Sharp distinctions between courses create different associations in the brain. You want the student to visualize how the training fits a goal.
- Arrange the seating in nontraditional format. The classroom setting brings too many old biases with it.

Urge your instructors to "meet" the people where they are *mentally*. This sounds easy, but it is not. Many trainers have preconceived notions of how an instructor or consultant should act. This often involves a formal posture and their best vocabulary. Instead, instructors should relax and share feelings about themselves. This builds an emotional bridge with the people, which helps the connection on more than a data exchange; it helps workers take ownership of the material and try it. In addition, the instructor's actions will be the role model for the bridging of emotions that is encouraged in the Golden Rule process.

SELLING THE NEED FOR TRAINING

Selling the need for training sounds like it ought to be a contradiction in terms. Certainly everyone wants training to move up in the organization so he or she can try new jobs, gain new skills, learn how to supervise, gain more production experience, etc. But that only happens in a utopian world. I have had many long talks with the responsible individuals from many organizations about the frustration we sometimes face in selling front-line supervisors on the need to receive training. We have shared our frustrations and nervous fears about supervisors agreeing to go to the classroom, and then hoping the trainer both is stunning in quality and possesses charisma.

Training cannot occur in a vacuum. It must come almost simultaneously in the beginning with some other events. These events include visible movements made by management to assure employees that this training energy will be a long-term change. Our supervisors have been subjected to many fads, to many top-level changes in philosophy. The supervisors tend to hold back to preserve their own sanity from another wild ride by top management that may stop suddenly at the first downturn in business or introduction of a new fad. Who can blame them for being cautious? To use training alone to begin a process of worker participation and cooperation can be like leading with your chin in a boxing match. There are many ways to achieve visible top management support, ranging from simple letters and memos to a presence in training, and from speeches and columns in the company newspaper to changes in the performance appraisal system that reinforced the use of the newly acquired skills.

> To use training alone to begin a process of worker participation and cooperation is like leading with your chin in a boxing match.

Front-line production supervisors don't always like training. Let's take a look at why it is difficult for some. In the very beginning they find that setting aside time for training a burden to balance: They have a product to produce; they are pushing people to work overtime; they rarely have backup supervisors; or they may have a tough union with which to deal. The last thing there is often time for is to be training for two, three, or more days. It may not be looked on as a gift or a bonus or a pat on the back. I'm not trying to promote a stereotype of the first-line person rejecting training outright. Rather, I'm just expressing in a realistic manner the problems they often face. In the true sense, most enjoy the classes and are pleased to learn ways to improve. They are able and very capable participants who are fun to teach.

Remember, be sure the supervisors are kept mentally moving. Use case studies, simulations, films, lecture, and games, weaving them through the curricula. Each person responds differently so the multiple approach is bound to "click."

> We must anchor training to achieve better results.

What we have noticed is that we must tie training to some other critical area of Golden Rule Management. I repeat—we must anchor training to achieve better results. We have to show how these skills we wish to impart in training are going to tie in with the mission of the organization. In other words, how are these new skills going to help me as a supervisor in accomplishing my job? Then we have to tie the new skills back into the performance appraisal system to encourage and reward the usage by the supervisors.

Training becomes a circle within the lines of Golden Rule Management. Training becomes like the highway to get to newer and greater heights of output, productivity, and quality, but we have to build the highway first. We have to take the time and effort to make the connection between all the money and effort spent in training to show very clearly how it is going to enhance the mission of the supervisor. After this is done, we start achieving commitment to the goals of training. Training now becomes a fast-track avenue in our organization, and it becomes a watershed for respect and dignity among our workers.

The formats used in training vary widely. We know there are group discussions, case studies, role play, films, lectures, and any combination of those. Certainly you need relevant hands-on types of arrangements to keep the employees' interest. But the format isn't as important, believe it or not, as making sure that people are sold on the importance of being in that room. To my chagrin and to anybody who has been involved in training over the years, if we don't sell people on the relevance of the skill we may never find out if they ever use the skills that we impart. The result is an intense network of frustration for the employees, the managers, and the trainers.

TOP MANAGEMENT CONNECTION

Consistent with the training of first-line supervisors is the optimum idea that we should, even if it is in capsule form, get the news across to the upper layers of management. They should know the area of training, who is being trained, the schedule of cross training, and the philosophy of training. They should visibly support training. Without this knowledge and support in place, and without the performance appraisal changes, top management can be a roadblock to any training. If they don't know and understand what is going on, their body language or indifferent verbal response can immediately negate progress. That is why some people suggest using a capsule summary for top management before starting training. The obvious question is why not start with upper level supervisors and train them first? That same question can be asked about everything. We can ask, for example, why not start with performance appraisal? Why not start with the mission statement? Why not start with cross training? Why not start with *whatever*? You cannot do everything first. Several things can be worked on simultaneously, but we are going to have to prioritize the organizational changeover to Golden Rule Management. Here, as in any place, there may be gaps. There may be discontinuity, because that is the nature of change in any organization. We can try to reduce the discontinuity and gaps, for example, by fitting capsule seminars into the program to at least make sure top management understands where the supervisors are going and what they plan to do with it.

How much time should be spent in training? The time spent in training can obviously vary widely. Recommendations range as high as twenty percent of a person's time on average should be spent in training. This figure correlates to the five percent of sales amount often quoted for the Japanese. This staggers the imagination when we first look at it. Senior managers and others might reply, "I might have to increase my work personnel by how many percentage points to cover this," let alone the dollar cost of training, the dollar cost of new employees, etc. For one thing, the percentage doesn't have to be that high. Others have already spent time trying to work out the problem of getting large numbers of individuals through training. At both the Hershey Chocolate and H. B. Reese Candy companies we used a team in training class and asked for their ideas on how we could train large numbers of people without totally disrupting the entire system. The workers did come up with an orderly process that seemed very workable. Did it take some sacrifices beyond the normal workloads? Did it take stretching themselves as individuals? Yes, but that is what we are looking for, that is the kind of excitement about the job and commitment to goals that we are hoping to achieve in individuals. All the members of these groups were sold on the importance of training to their own lives and how it would enhance their abilities to accomplish the companies' missions and objectives. They saw training as a necessary component of life, and they produced some very creative ideas. There is always a trade-off point beyond which more training doesn't enhance the quality or the output of the organization. No one has found that optimum point yet. Currently some people agree but others disagree with the twenty percent mark. It is very difficult to launch from zero to twenty percent. The process should be more like a step-wise progression. Also, training should be an average figure, meaning every week we will not have X number of hours spent somewhere. Remember, not all training is away from the job or our plant. Much can be accomplished by cross-training and on-the-job training, both utilizing coaching techniques for learning. Many U.S. executives could become task oriented and end up just making up training activities to keep us busy in order to meet our twenty percent figure goals. We do not want to get tied up in those kinds of numbers games. We still want to keep the experience, time, and quality of the training meaningful.

TRAINING IN DEEPER WISDOM

The concept of training in a deeper wisdom confuses many top to first-line managers. The first thoughts that arise are extreme ones about "religious" teaching, and Title VII religious accommodations. This worry and misinformation results in the virtual exclusion of this form of training from our corporate world. Yet the values gained from this training are those we prize in workers. Such values include:

- Teamwork or being a team player
- Responsibility for one's self and one's work
- Perseverance
- Understanding the balance of job reality and life reality.

Training in a deeper form of wisdom is also called spirituality. Spiritualism is not religious teaching. Religions are defined as a shared set of social beliefs, ideas, and actions that connect to those "things" that cannot be empirically held as true. These "things" affect the course of natural and human events and actions (Terpstra and David 1985).

There is readily documented use of spiritual training in corporate Japan. In one such program, two-thirds of total training time was devoted to technical and managerial skills, the remaining third emphasized spiritualism. The goal of spiritualism is to encourage pride and respect for work. The student learns the viewpoint of the organization, its competitive circumstance, and its intention to contribute to the social good. The various categories that training in spiritualism embodies are as follows:

- Stress reduction techniques help reduce anxiety. The result is more efficient work and the ability to focus. Stress reduction techniques typically employ meditation, deep breathing, and/or self-hypnosis. The process here teaches workers to look to themselves to find solutions. Working together with shared values is important. Our own growth means being less selfish and more helpful to others.

- Give time and energy on a volunteer basis to someone else. This can be to charity groups or another organization. The lesson received helps define the meaning of work, and the rewards of work depend on our positive attitude.

- All work is meaningful and has dignity in a task well done. This is critical for us. Some jobs are repetitive and dull, yet each is vital for the success of our mission.

- In the Japanese experience, time is spent participating in military drills to learn discipline and group order and cooperation. In addition, time is spent in a farming environment to learn the lesson of persistence and hard work with the reward at the end when the crop is harvested. The self-reliant nature and ingenuity of farmers is a valued lesson for most corporate students. We need not run to boot camp or to an Iowa farm to seek these core values. Yet the values of perseverance, self-reliance, discipline, and composure are valuable. There are a number of retreats that can convey the same results (Terpstra and David 1985).

The concept of spiritual training helps the employee learn balance in life through the creation of a stable mind free from confusion and frustration. Spiritual training uses real events and life experiences, not religious "truths" or "things," to gain this result. Therefore, we avoid the problems inherent with incorporating religious values.

Tips you can use for training in spiritualism follow. This is not an exhaustive list. The dialogue used should reflect the culture of the organization.

Tips for Spiritualism Training

- Employ training in mental reframing to change to and keep a positive mental outlook about work and life.

- Teach stress reduction techniques. My wife taught stress management techniques to the entire work force at one plant. Reducing anxiety is the first step toward feeling balanced in life.

- Use team building exercises that embody the message of harmony and shared goals. This goes beyond conflict resolution training and the typical team building menu of topics. It brings us to the acceptance of conflict as natural and how to channel the energy of conflict in pursuit of our mission.

- Create trust building exercises. These games have an easy transition to the job. The lack of trust is a major issue in retarding the growth of teamwork and shared values in our organizations. Exercises that help build this take us away from feelings of vulnerability to feelings of openness, which translates quickly into better communications. Books such as *Games Trainers Play* (Newstrom and Scannell, 1980) are full of exercises for this area. No, you do not need a trained psychologist or full-time consultant. You can do this. It's a slow process in trust building. A four-hour session with a consultant is not the only road to follow. That has been tried and what can result are smiles and warm fuzzy feelings in the session and no transference to the job. Another idea is frequent one-hour exercises and group exchanges, or an introductory session with a good consultant and a plan to continue the program of trust building.

There is certainly strong evidence that spiritual training could become a part of our corporate life. A resurgence of spirituality is now happening. There is an undercurrent of feeling that our corporate world lacks a philosophy and ethical base. This void often discourages and confuses many employees. Spirituality with its shared values can be useful to bring a value base to our jobs. Remember, using shared values is considered the preferred way to handle difficult topics such as sexual harassment, physical disabilities, and race or religious discrimination. Shared values do not use difficult do or don't lists or complex legal jargon, as often shows up in our policy manuals. Shared values teach a sense of respect and dignity for every person, which is a good bridge to achieve commitment to quality.

CAREER PATHS

Does training tie into the career path of an individual in an organization? We have indicated in discussion of the performance appraisal that careers and career paths certainly have a significant impact on an individual's life and feelings of self-esteem. There is certainly a very close tie-in between training and career paths, and if we can make the tie-in more direct, then we can get another level of commitment to the organizational goals. That is, not all training will necessarily be directed to the individual's career aspirations in the future. Some may be tied directly to current work needs or work environment problems. But, if we can also tie in so that the training will enhance and progress the individual along their own career paths, then we do provide an access point toward worker motivation. This effort will partially tie in to auxiliary levels of commitment to the organization. If nothing else, it adds to the psychology of knowing that I am progressing as an individual.

It is no secret that many individuals do not take full advantage of all career path opportunities in organizations where they are present. What is also amazing are the individuals who do not take advantage of career path opportunities that still have a higher output level. The reason for this seems to be the knowledge and comfort that these avenues are available should the employee decide to go in that direction.

Career paths need to be written, or at least well understood. They are a powerful tie to respect for people. "Written" means we have documented at least the key job areas and how one can progress to them by acquiring new skills. Yes, we do want to encourage new skill acquisitions. Growth is a necessary component for people. We don't hover in place at a certain skill level for life. You are either going forward or you are going backward. Just the pace of technology change can make a mechanic's job obsolete every four or five years if they are not receiving more training. No job is an exception. We are fooling ourselves if we are not involved in some form of self-improvement. It takes a reasonable amount of effort just to keep up and, in effect, keeping up is actually going forward.

This is one reason we do not discourage courses of study not directly job related. The reality is that the employees' job efficiency and productivity will still be improved. The correlation between career paths and productivity is very positive even when the career path is away from our company. While the employees remain with us, their output is high and quality is good.

Chapter 11

BEING A POSITIVE SUPERVISOR IN A NON–GOLDEN RULE MANAGEMENT ORGANIZATION

There is another aspect to successful Golden Rule Management. Like so many points we have talked about, it is more glue that brings the process together. This vital point is attitude, more specifically, a *positive attitude*. From Norman Vincent Peale to Peter Drucker, positive attitudes are factors that have been emphasized in achieving success—not only in our businesses, but in the balance of our life.

Writings that deal with positivism and teaching are filled with examples where instructor perceptions of ability have clouded the reality. The generic story goes like this:

> An otherwise similar group of people (experiments have ranged from college, adult education, factory training to grade school) are divided into two groups. Call them groups 1 and 2. The instructor for group 1 is told this group is very smart, motivated, and trustworthy. The instructor for group 2 is told this group lacks motivation and is not especially intelligent. Remember, both groups 1 and 2 are really the same, just randomly divided for the experiment. Yet in almost every case the results turn out that group 1 excels on the tests, their classes are alive with discussion, and both students and teacher look forward to the classes. Group 2 students fare poorly, and both students and teacher find it difficult to come to class.

The negative perception by group 2 of the teacher's attitude becomes a self-fulfilling prophecy. Likewise, the positive attitude and approach to group 1 becomes self-fulfilling. This is not a new idea, yet we regularly repeat the errors of negative inference on groups. This reflects our management system of both rewards and punishment that is based on negative reinforcement. That is, failure is punished, and success only avoids punishment. We need not look far for examples, a bonus is just another negative system reward soon forgotten.

Golden Rule Management is alive with positive feelings and attitudes. The first-line supervisors and workers have high regard and praise for the programs. Yet the major obstacle to the spread of this concept is not with the worker or union. It is with upper management, who retain negative attitudes toward the program. Negative attitudes toward any program, whether it is quality circles, employee involvement, or whatever, are a problem. The reasons vary, and are not without empathy and understanding on our part. However, the reasons can be overcome with education about employee participation. Like anything in life, a new philosophy presents uncertainty. Despite their lofty titles and salary, top managers rarely react differently to change than anybody else. What they don't know causes discomfort. They may camouflage it better, be articulate in hiding their fears, but the result is the same.

FAILURE TO BE POSITIVE

We have all read articles that discuss and list the many reasons worker participation fails. The lists, when examined, focus on the negative aspects of people. Failure to be positive about people and the outcomes they can generate was a topic of concern for Peter Drucker:

> A man should never be appointed to a managerial position if his vision focuses on people's weaknesses rather than on their strengths. The man who knows what people cannot do, but never sees anything they can do will undermine the spirit of the organization. (Drucker 1973)

Various authors list areas that present major obstacles to participative management and quality circles:

Obstacles to Positive Management
- Not including the entire organization in these programs
- Time span too short to judge success
- Resistance to decentralization and sharing of decision-making
- Preventing regular participation by the unions.

Not Including the Entire Organization

Spot testing of ideas is a common method used to work out the problems in a system before total implementation, but it should be given company-wide treatment as soon as possible. The negative implications to the work force by partial use of a participative setting are large and may seriously hurt future implementation attempts. Workers frequently complain that top management only preaches participation. The first-line supervisors have been trained for it. But no one trained or told the mid-level group about the vision or sold them on the idea and so they kill off the process.

Failure to Decentralize and Use Shared Decisions

The resistance to decentralization and sharing of decision-making is a problem that dates back to the roots of our economic system. Many writers have offered themes about its origins, ranging from the protestant work ethic to capitalism. All are to some extent correct. However, U.S. managers continue to find that giving up power is difficult. Yet most of the major successful U.S. organizations realize the positive effects gained by acknowledging what good things the employees can do for the organization. Peter Drucker acknowledged the strength of sharing and the positive results of having employees involved in decision-making twenty years ago:

> A manager must treat the people with whom he works as a resource to himself . . . to look to them for guidance regarding his own job . . . to demand of them that they accept it as their responsibility to enable their manager to do a better and more effective job. The manager needs to build upward responsibility and upward contribution into the job of each subordinate. (Drucker 1973)

A positive attitude allows the freedom and confidence to share the decisions. It sends the message to the employees that "I believe in you," "You are a good worker," "I will benefit from your input and so will the organization." Both the manager and the employee grow in these circumstances. The net effect is an adult-like, business-like reaction from employees.

The tight controls on decision-making have their origins in negative attitudes. For example, the feeling that the people who work for you are not "OK," that they may not be intelligent enough to make sound decisions. The manager with the negative view says, "I will manage people by taking away their dignity," and does so by always holding out rewards. For example, the employees are kept "mindlessly" working and their enthusiasm is kept up by using the bonus or annual raise approach. Many participative programs have failed because monetary rewards were used as the key component to gain group commitment. These degenerate into compensation schemes and no longer function as an outlet for creativity and sharing of decision-making. Back in the 1970s, Peter Drucker warned that the era of this attitude was soon to end:

> Today, affluence and . . . rising education of the middle class threaten to deprive the sovereign (manager) of his carrot-and-stick approach. (Drucker 1973)

Failure to Include Unions

Keeping unions from participative activities is like the ostrich burying its head in the sand. Unions may elect not to be a part of any program. For managers to ban union participation unilaterally is a signal to the workers that unions are unacceptable. The message means workers are also not OK since they belong to the union. Such actions reduce the chances of gaining employee commitment.

Being positive is a learned response, just as being negative is a learned response. Yet focusing on the negative does not foster creative ideas or solutions. It doesn't matter if it's autos rolling down an assembly line or ideas from a think tank, positive attitudes foster increased productivity. They also enrich our work life and our general feelings of well being.

POINTS TO REMEMBER

Many means are available for us to be positive and help use positivism on the job, but the main ways used with success are given in the following list. This list is certainly not all-inclusive, but the ideas given are ones successfully used by first-line supervisors over time. That in itself lends credence to their use.

Ways to Use Positivism on the Job

- Do not allow a negative statement unless the person has a possible solution. Complaining does not solve problems, it only heightens the negative.
- If you are "going it alone" as a supervisor, you will find your consistent positive responses and smiles will rub off on your employees. It will not be long until your boss will want to know what you are doing to raise the morale of the people.
- Try to restate aggressive or conflict-like statements made to you as problem issues to be solved with opportunities for growth. The results will be dramatic.
- Try games to turn around the negative. Have a meeting to list the "worst things." For example, if you want to improve customer relations,

have everyone offer ideas to make customer relations worse. Yes, worse. The result is a lively, creative, and humorous discussion of ideas that emerge.

- Have employees complete the phrase "Given the chance, I would write _____ on the employee bulletin board for all to read." Besides being therapeutic in allowing people to vent, it also has an element of humor. Humor adds greatly to the atmosphere of work. It reduces stress and anxiety and helps keep a proper work environment and perspective.

If some areas we indicated earlier are changed to proactive policies and statements, the attitude of all involved will be markedly different:

Positivism Pointers

- All of us can benefit from Golden Rule Management.
- Sharing leadership makes each one of us a proactive supervisor for change.
- We each can make good decisions from our areas of knowledge.
- If you already have a union, then view it as adding value to the atmosphere.
- Be upbeat in describing these programs to other managers and employees.
- Visualize success and discuss the positive future impact this may have on your organization. At the Rhor Industries plant in Hagerstown, Maryland, a course on being positive was regularly taught to new employees. At the H. B. Reese Company, positivism is a course that is part of the supervisory development program.
- Be positive about your organization, positive about your job, and positive about yourself. Believe you are the key to everyone's success, irrespective of the job.
- As negative thoughts about yourself and others on the job enter your mind, try yelling "Stop" (to yourself, of course). This has the effect of interrupting this damaging self-talk.
- Start each day with a positive idea. Recheck yourself several times during the day to keep restating the positive thought. This keeps those inevitable minor upsets from becoming our main line of thought.

Changing old habits is not easy, especially when most of our managerial structures are geared toward negative reinforcement. Yet the apparent edge toward success that is offered by being positive makes the change in behavior worthwhile. The end result is a work force that is excited about their jobs. This is more appealing than one that is despondent from a failure to participate in the organization's success.

Why not close this idea with a quote from the leader in positive thinking, Norman Vincent Peale:

> Positive thinkers are bound to be positive doers. They are achievers and winners, and I have noted that they also have non-irritating though strong personalities. The literature eludes to this power and its uses are limitless. Positivism is a learned response. (Peale 1984)

The Golden Rule process is a very simple concept. Treat others in the manner you wish to be treated—with respect, dignity, and adult-like actions. As described here, it can be instituted organization wide or by each individual supervisor. No matter what the scale of usage, each degree of practice makes things better.

Chapter 12

PULLING IT TOGETHER

We have spent a great deal of time examining many aspects of Golden Rule Management. Our topics of coverage showed how to proceed with a conversion to a Golden Rule environment. The optimum is for the whole work unit to change, but reality is often somewhat different. You may be "going it alone" in your own local work group—which is fine. Many things can be done individually. Treating people as you wish to be treated will be effective in any dimension or magnitude. Remember, one person can make a difference. The road map for this program shows the stepping stones to progress:

A Road Map for Golden Rule Progression

- Change our organizations to efficient units that are lean in hierarchy and yet don't adversely affect product quality or service.

- Make our supervisors facilitators of the human resource component and not fire fighters. The person becomes the expert.

- Turn the information flow so that the critical information on elements is usable at the operating level and flows up.

- Personalize the goals of the organization so that everyone knows his or her role in achieving success.

- Gain multiple levels of employee commitment to achieve quality service, excellence, productivity, and make work a source of personal creativity.

- Build self-esteem in workers and at the same time achieve product quality improvements. Both sides win.

- Anchor training to skills, values, and the organizational mission to achieve higher results.

- Turn performance appraisals into "performance getting" sessions.

- Use emotion as a positive tool for supervisors and build it into interpersonal skills that emphasize these for the benefit of the worker.

- Make the philosophy the key to your change.
- Rely on more than technical training.

Let's look at an example to help sum up this thought. It is about a former retail store employee who quit because of the treatment he received. His words to me were "A manager of a competing store always treats me better than my boss. He greets me with a smile, a pat on my back. He makes me feel good and important, the way I thought my boss should make me feel."

No one should get lost in the "how to's" lest they become hard and fast. The examples are only guides to implement the philosophy.

THE PHILOSOPHY

The philosophy is respect and dignity for workers, adult-like treatment and letting go of unnecessary rules and controls. Always use positive terms to deal with people. If someone makes a mistake, focus your remarks on how you would see the job done well, not on the mistake. In essence, treat others as you wish to be treated.

The philosophy is the frame of reference to keep. I have found that each organization is unique and we must alter the "how to's" to suit each culture. Let's acquire the feeling of being "with people" in a new way and not relying on hard and fast rules. We must be flexible, not set in our ways.

Philosophy is important to any organization. It is the spirit of being that gives definition to an organization. A modern day business philosopher describes business philosophy as how we really run a business and no organization is an exception.

> A business without a philosophy is a business without guidelines for defining its purpose and values. It is an unexamined business. In other words, a business that lives only for survival, only for the bottom line. This is the kind of place that takes away the joy of living—even if we do make money. (Azevedo 1985)

Golden Rule Management is a philosophy of "corporate self" in dealing with people. It does not go into hard concepts of accounting, finance, or law. Yet, it is the soft interpersonal philosophy that is lacking in so many organizations. Few of the organizations I work with have trouble with the economics of business. Most have good training in the technical aspects of quality. Yet many continue to have difficulty in achieving the type of employee response they envisioned. For many organizations, training in worker participation is deep in technical aspects but fails to go into the philosophy that governs the process. The philosophy is the "software" that helps the system make "sense" to the worker.

I have taught worker participation for years, including courses on how to handle conflict, handling data, how to run a meeting, and how to make a presentation. These are good and necessary skills, they need to be acquired. But it is like the hard accounting and finance stuff—we feel if we understand the mechanics the rest will come. That is not so.

THE ORGANIZATION SPEAKS

In our work life there are many examples of how our organization reflects its attitude, how it tells customers and employees where the priorities lie. General Dynamics appears to make itself clear. Their priorities appear to be stock analysts and Wall Street traders. The top executives received a $15.2 million dollar bonus under a plan in which the executives received a bonus if stock prices averaged $10 above the February 15 level and stayed there for ten trading days. Get this, for each subsequent $10 increase, managers received bonuses equal to twice their base salary. My knowledge of General Dynamics and its plan is from the financial section of a newspaper, the *San Diego Union*, which makes it perfect to report my impression. I am not a biased insider, just another observer. What is observed is that product quality didn't trigger the bonus, positive changes in worker morale didn't trigger the bonus. This sends a clear message of priorities. It becomes even more clear when we realize that the same day the company adopted the program it disclosed plans to lay off up to thirty percent of its workers over four years. This story sends a clear message. It says the employee and the products they make are a low priority.

The industrialist who feels compelled to make all the decisions and kills off worker enthusiasm with toughly worded direct orders sets philosophy and priorities in a negative way.

Golden Rule Management sets a tone that is unmistakable. The priorities and philosophy toward people ring out clearly. All employees are of value. With you, the employee, we will achieve our goals.

THE BATTLE FOR SURVIVAL

Organizations are engaged in life and death struggles. Social agencies struggle with the budget ax, banks and other financial institutions struggle with the rapidly changing world in which they exist, others struggle with the world of international competition. The struggle has moved into areas we are not fond of engaging.

The world of nonprice competition is where the Japanese have waged battle and appear to be in the lead. Gas mileage is an example. U.S. auto companies competed on gas mileage by making everything inside the car plastic, and hence lighter, but it made U.S. cars seem cheap. Japanese companies recognized this and became aerodynamically efficient instead of using plastic. To take the focus off the low price, low quality analogy, they emphasized quality, not just price.

Reduction of cycle time would result in an edge in the nonprice competition area. U.S. executives knew this but failed to respond. Cooperative work relationships make the employee a partner in finding this edge. It means entering a new level of understanding, which is hard. To reduce cycle time, Japanese practice a setup on machinery like a race car crew practices its "pit stop" routines. We never took this approach. We kept to the hard facts and never engaged the worker as a partner. Top executives get massive bonuses for short-term thinking such as easy fixes like cutting R&D, or capital expenditures, or laying off workers. Several years later the company is typically in worse shape than before. The miracle short-term fix didn't do a thing for reduction of cycle time or the nonprice areas of importance.

Our companies are now starting to recognize this; the emphasis on just-in-time inventory and quality reinforce this. Many are struggling for a new title for bosses. They vary from coach, to facilitator, to unboss, to leader. The search is frantic. It's a search for a new buzz word or a quick fix. The truth is, we need a philosophy of organization life. We glare at the Japanese and Germans and say their people and culture are "different" from ours. The reality is they have a philosophy that emphasizes a core set of values the worker can commit to and simultaneously emphasize product quality. Golden Rule Management can offer this same advantage to U.S. workers and companies.

There is no doubt that we could once again become a major contender in world competition. But the journey has to begin with people. It needs to begin with a new expression of how we feel about them and treat them. It needs to involve people that are balanced in their outlook to life and work. Golden Rule Management can be a vehicle to achieve balance and harmony. The components of respect and dignity are basic concepts. Adult-like treatment is consistent with our values and beliefs. Our workers and supervisors want to succeed. All that is left for us is to begin the journey.

References and Additional Reading

The following books, magazines, and newspaper articles were used as references in the writing of this book. In addition, some selections are presented for those who wish to pursue other avenues of thought on topics we discussed.

American Productivity Center. August 1985. *White Collar Productivity Improvement.* Houston, Texas: The American Productivity Center.

American Psychological Association. August 1985. *Monitor,* Vol. 16, p. 22.

Anderson, Carl R. 1984. *Management: Skills, Functions, and Organization Performance.* Dubuque, Iowa: William C. Brown.

Argyris, Chris. 1957. *Personality and Organization.* New York: Harper and Brothers, pp. 47–53.

Atkinson, Lynn, and Christopher Hyatt. 1988. *Power and Empowerment: The Power Principle.* Las Vegas, Nevada: Falcon Press.

Azevedo, Americ. December 1985. "The Importance of Philosophy to Business." *Bay Area Business Magazine,* Vol. IV, No. 5.

Baldwin, Bruce A. March 1985. "Burning Out in America." *Piedmont Airlines.* pp. 11–14.

Barbee, Cliff, and Valerie Bott. 1991. "Customer Treatment as a Mirror of Employee Treatment." *SAM Advanced Management Journal,* Vol. 56, No. 2 (Spring), pp. 27–32.

Beatty, R. S., and C. S. Scheneier. 1981. *Personnel Administration.* 2nd ed. Reading, Massachusetts: Addison-Wesley Publishing Company.

Beinecke, Richard H. January 19, 1984. "The Costs of Mental Health and Substance Abuse." *Health Industries of American Report,* pp. 25–26.

Belasco, James A. 1991. *Teaching the Elephant to Dance,* New York: Plume.

Bell, C. R. October 1987. "Criteria for Selecting Instructional Strategies." *Training and Development Journal,* Vol. 31, No. 10, pp. 3–7.

Blanchard, Ken. June 1991. "Situational View of Leadership." *Executive Excellence,* Vol. 8, No. 6, pp. 22–23.

Bureau of Labor Statistics. April 1982. *Productivity Measures for Selected Industries, 1954–80.* Washington, DC: U.S. Department of Labor, Bulletin 2128, p. 2.

Cabrera, James C. September 1990. "Proactive Career Management." *Executive Excellence,* Vol. 7, No. 9, pp. 17–18.

Carnevale, Anthony Patrick. January 1986. "The Learning Enterprise." *Training and Development Journal*.

Casey, F. M. 1979. *Work Attitudes and Work Experience*. Washington, DC: U.S. Department of Labor, Research and Development Monograph 60.

Constanzaro, J. L. 1976. "Selecting a Career Path." *Personnel Journal*, Vol. 55, pp. 330–331.

Cordery, John L., Walter S. Mueller, and Leigh M. Smith. June 1991. "Attitudinal and Behavioral Effects of Autonomous Group Working: A Longitudinal Field Study." *Academy of Management Journal*, Vol. 34, No. 2, pp. 464–476.

Cristiani, T. S., and M. F. Cristiani. 1979. "The Application of Counseling Skills in the Business and Industrial Setting." *The Personnel and Guidance Journal*, Vol. 58, pp. 166–169.

Darling, John R. July 1990. "Team Building in the Small Business Firm." *Journal of Small Business Management*, Vol. 28, No. 3, pp. 86–91.

DeCenzo, David A., and Stephen Holoviak. 1990. *Employee Benefits*. Englewood Cliffs, New Jersey: Prentice Hall, Chaps. 4, 10, and 11.

DeCenzo, David, and Stephen Robbins. 1988. *Personnel/Human Resource Management*. Englewood Cliffs, New Jersey: Prentice Hall.

Dewer, Donald. 1980. *The Quality Circle: What You Should Know About It*. Los Angeles, California: Quality Circle Institute.

Dick, William M. 1972. *Labor and Socialism in America*. Port Washington, New York: Kennikat Press.

Donovan, Michael. 1989. "Employees Who Manage Themselves." Proceedings 11th Annual Conference, Association for Quality and Participation, Kansas City, Missouri, pp. 112–119.

Drucker, Peter F. November 26, 1985. "How to Measure White Collar Productivity." *The Wall Street Journal*.

Drucker, Peter F. 1973. *Management*. New York: Harper and Row.

Eng, J. E., and J. S. Gottsdanker. January 1979. "Positive Changes from a Career Development Program." *Training and Development Journal*, pp. 3–6.

Ewing, D. W. 1981. "Who Wants Corporate Democracy?" *Harvard Business Review*, Spring.

Falricant, A. 1981. "The Productivity Issue: An Overview," *Productivity Prospects for Growth*, edited by J. M. Rosow. New York: D. Van Nostrand.

Feingold, S. N. 1971. *Occupational Counseling in Industry: The Encyclopedia of Education*. New York: MacMillan.

Fiedler, Fred E., and Joseph E. Garcia. March 1985. "Comparing Organization Development and Management Training." *Personnel Administrator*, p. 36.

Field, Lloyd. March 1991. "Participative Management—All Together Now." *Canadian Manager*, Vol. 16, No. 1, pp. 14–15, 25.

Fisher, Joann. 1985. "Secretaries Speak Up for Training." *Office Skills Training Report*, McGraw-Hill Training Systems Publication, No. 4, Spring.

Fournier, F. F. 1978. *Coaching for Improved Work Performance*. 2nd ed. Englewood Cliffs, New Jersey: Prentice-Hall.

Foxman, Loretta D., and Walter L. Polsky. May 1991. "HR Skills Help Managers Turn Around Poor Performers." *Personnel Journal*, Vol. 70, No. 5, pp. 28–31.

Fritz, Roger. June 1991. "I'm Your Boss . . . Why Are You Laughing?" *Supervisory Management*, Vol. 36, No. 6, pp. 10–11.

Gitlow, Abraham L. 1986. *Labor and Industrial Society*. Homewood, Illinois: Robert D. Irwin.

Glicken, Morely D. April 28, 1985. "Don't Let Office Stress Become Your Worst Enemy." *National Business Employment Weekly*, p. 7.

Gorlin, Harriet, and Schein, Lawrence. 1984. *Innovations in Managing Human Resources*, New York: The Conference Board, Inc., Conference Board Report No. 849.

Gould, S. 1978. "Career Planning in the Organization." *Human Resource Management*, Spring, pp. 8–11.

Grayson, David. 1991. "Self-Regulating Work Groups—An Aspect of Organizational Change." *International Journal of Manpower* (UK), Vol. 12, No. 1, pp. 22–29.

Hamlin, Richard. April 1991. "A Practical Guide to Empowering Your Employees." *Supervisory Management*, Vol. 36, No. 4, p. 8.

Hammer, W. C., and F. J. Smith. 1978. "Work Attitudes as Predicators of Unionization Activity." *Journal of Applied Psychology*, Vol. 4, pp. 415–421.

Hampden-Turner, Charles. 1970. *Radical Man: The Process of Psycho-Social Development*. Cambridge, Massachusetts: Schenkman Publishing Company.

Hand, H. H., and J. W. Solcum. 1972. "A Longitudinal Study of the Effects of Human Relations Training on Managerial Effectiveness." *Journal of Applied Psychology*, Vol. 56, pp. 412–417.

Hautaluoma, J. E., and J. F. Gavin. 1975. "Effects of Organizational Diagnosis and Intervention on Blue Collar Blues." *Journal of Applied Behavior Science*, Vol. 11, pp. 475–596.

Henderson, Richard I. 1985. *Compensation Management and Rewarding Performance*, 4th ed. Reston, Virginia: Reston Publishing Company.

Higgins, James. 1982. *Human Relations: Concepts and Skills*. New York: Random House.

Hillman, Larry W., David R. Schwandt, and David E. Bartz. 1990. "Enhancing Staff Members' Performance Through Feedback and Coaching." *Journal of Management Development* (UK) Vol. 9, No. 3, pp. 20–27.

Hoeir, John. April 30, 1990. "The Strange Bedfellows Backing Workplace Reform," *Business Week*, p. S7.

Holly, William, and Kenneth Jennings. 1984. *The Labor Relations Process.* New York: Dryden Press.

Holoviak, Stephen J. October 1990. "Compensation That Attracts and Retains Employees in Small Business." *NBDC Report* (Nebraska Business Development Center), No. 119.

Holoviak, Stephen J. 1984a. *Costing Labor Contracts and Judging Their Financial Impact.* New York: Praeger.

Holoviak, Stephen J. October 1984b. "Career Planning—A Link to Better Productivity." *Performance and Instruction Journal,* Vol. 23, No. 7, pp. 7–8.

Holoviak, Stephen J. June 1982. "The Impact of Training on Company Productivity Levels." *Performance and Instruction Journal,* Vol. 21, No. 5, pp. 6–8.

Holoviak, Stephen J., David A. Decenzo, and Sharon Brookens Holoviak. April 1985. "Assess the Needs for Counseling Education Among Industrial Personnel." *Performance and Instruction,* Vol. 24, pp. 1–5.

Holoviak, Stephen J., and Sharon Brookens Holoviak. April 1989. "Negative Attitudes and Quality Circles." *Quality Digest,* pp. 79–84.

Holoviak, Stephen J., and Sharon Brookens Holoviak. July–August 1984. "The Benefits of In-House Counseling." *Personnel,* Vol. 61, No. 4, pp. 53–59.

Holoviak, Stephen J., and Susan S. Sipkoff. 1987. *Managing Human Productivity: People Are Your Best Investments.* New York: Praeger, Chaps. 2, 4, 5 and 6.

Huberman, John. July–August 1964. "Discipline, Not Punishment." *Harvest Business Review,* pp. 62–68.

Kellogg, Marion. 1975. *What to Do About Performance Appraisal,* revised ed., AMACOM American Management Association, pp. 20, 39, 99, 114, 151.

Kelly, John, and Caroline Kelly. March 1991. "Them and Us: Social Psychology and the New Industrial Relations." *British Journal of Industrial Relations* (UK) Vol. 29, No. 1, pp. 25–49.

Kets de Vires, M. F. R., and Danny Miller. 1987. *The Neurotic Organization: Diagnosing and Changing Counterproductive Styles of Management.* San Francisco: Jossey-Bass Publishers.

Kezsbom, Deborah S. October 1990. "Are You Really Ready to Build a Project Team?" *Industrial Engineering,* Vol. 22, No. 10, pp. 50–55.

Kiecheel, Walter. November 4, 1991. "The Boss as Coach." *Fortune,* p. 201.

Kirby, Paula, and S. J. Holoviak. April 1985. "Evaluating Quality Circle Programs." *1985 International Quality Circle Annual Conference Transactions,* Cincinnati, Ohio, IAQC, pp. 157–160.

Kochan, Thomas. 1980. *Collective Bargaining and Industrial Relations.* Homewood, Illinois: Richard D. Irwin.

LaGreca, Genevieve. September 1985. "The Stress You Make." *Personnel Journal,* p. 43.

Lee, Chris. June 1990. "Beyond Teamwork." *Training*, Vol. 27, No. 6, pp. 25–34.

Likert, Rensis. July–August 1959. "Motivational Approach to Management Development." *Harvard Business Review*, p. 75.

List, Charles E. September 1982. "How to Make Quality Circles Work for Your Organization." *Personnel Journal*, pp. 652–654.

Lusterman, Seymour. 1985. *Trends in Corporate Education and Training*, New York: The Conference Board, Inc., Conference Board Report No. 870.

McCune, Jenny. October 1990. "Consensus Builder." *Success*, Vol. 37, No. 8, pp. 42–45.

McGregor, Douglas. May–June 1957. "An Uneasy Look at Performance Appraisal." *Harvard Business Review*, p. 90.

Meyers, Diana T. 1987. "Work and Self-Respect." *Moral Rights in the Workplace*, edited by Gertrude Ezorosky. Albany, New York: State University Press of New York, p. 18.

Milbourn, Gene, Jr. April–June 1984. "Alcoholism, Drug Abuse, Job Stress: What Small Business Can Do." *American Journal of Small Business*, Vol. 8, pp. 36–48.

Miles, J. B. February 1985. "How to Help Troubled Workers." *Computer Decisions*, Vol. 17, pp. 66–67.

Mroczkowski, Tomasz. June 1984. "Quality Circles, Fine—What Next?" *Personnel Administrator*.

Naisbett, John. 1984. *Megatrends*. New York: Warner Books.

Nandyal, Ray K., and Dave Welch. June 1991. "Goals—Orientation, SPC, and Incentives." *Quality*, Vol. 30, No. 6, pp. Q12–Q14.

Nellis, David. April 1984. "Starting and Developing Quality Circles." *1985 IAQC Annual Conference Transactions*, Cincinnati, Ohio, IAQC, pp. 337–339.

New York Stock Exchange, Office of Economic Research. 1982. *People and Productivity: A Challenge to Corporate America*. New York: New York Stock Exchange.

New York Times. March 18, 1985. "Japanese Companies in the U.S. Seen Excelling."

Newstrom, John, and Edward Scannell. 1980. *Games Trainers Play*. New York: McGraw-Hill.

Niehouse, Olivia L. July 1984. "Measuring Your Burnout Potential." *Supervising Management*, pp. 29–31.

Odione, George S. January 1985. "Human Resource Strategies for the '80s." *Training*, p. 49.

Oswald, Rudy. 1981. "Unions and Productivity." *Productivity: Prospects for Growth*, edited by Jerome M. Rosow. New York: D. Van Nostrand, pp. 98–99.

Ottele, Richard G., and Barbara A. Schaefer. January 1991. "How to Provide Effective On-the-Job Coaching for Your Staff." *Practical Accountant*, Vol. 24, No. 1, pp. 70–73.

Peale, Norman Vincent. 1987. *Power of the Plus Factor*. New York: Fawcett Crest.

Persico, John Jr., Betty L. Bednarczyk, and David P. Negus. January 1990. "Three Routes to the Same Destination: TQM (Part 1)." *Quality Progress*, Vol. 23, No. 1, pp. 29–33.

"The Power of Excellence and Quality." April 17, 1990. *Forbes.*

Richardson, Peter R. 1985. "Courting Greater Employee Involvement Through Participative Management." *Sloan Management Review*, Winter.

Rigdon, Joan E. October 19, 1990. "Team Builders Shine in Perilous Waters." *Wall Street Journal*, p. B1.

Roehm, Harper A., Donald J. Klein, and Joseph F. Castellano. March 1991. "Springing to World-Class Manufacturing." *Management Accounting*, Vol. 72, No. 9, pp. 40–44.

Rohan, Thomas M. January 21, 1991. "War and Now Peace in Toledo." *Industry Week*, Vol. 240, No. 2, pp. 54–61.

Rosow, J. M. 1979. "Quality of Work-life Issues in the 1980s," *Work in America the Decade Ahead*, edited by C. Kerr and J. M. Rosow. New York: D. Van Nostrand.

Schuster, Frederick. 1985. *Human Resources Management: Concepts, Cares, and Readings*. 2nd ed. Reston, Virginia: Reston Publishing Company.

Sheridan, John H. August 6, 1990. "World-Class Manufacturing: Lessons from the Gurus." *Industry Week*, Vol. 239, No. 15, pp. 35–41.

Shneider, Susan. 1991. "Managing Boundaries in Organizations," *Organizations on the Couch: Clinical Perspectives on Organizational Behavior and Change*, edited by Manfred F. R. Kets de Vires. San Francisco: Jossey-Bass Publishers, pp. 109–150.

Smith, Frederick W. January 1991. "Empowering Employees." *Small Business Reports*, Vol. 16, No. 1, pp. 15–20.

Spayd, Elizabeth. April 15, 1990. "Service Firms Cheer the Team Concept." *Washington Post.*

Sperry Corporation. 1983. *Quality Circle Training Program: Facilitator Manual*. Princeton, New Jersey: Sperry Corporation.

Staudohar, Paul D., and Holly E. Brown. 1987. *Deindustrialization and Plant Closure*. Robert Z. Lawrence, "Is Deindustrialization a Myth?" Lexington, Massachusetts: Lexington Books, pp. 25–39.

Suchan, James, and Clyde Scott. November 1984. "Readability Levels of Collective Bargaining Agreements." *Personnel Administrator*, Vol. 29, No. 11, pp. 73–80.

Sutcliff, Jon, and Jay Schuster. September 1985. "Benefits Revisited, Benefits Predicted." *Personnel Journal*, p. 62.

Suters, Everett T. February 1991. "Inspirational Management." *Executive Excellence*, Vol. 8, No. 2, pp. 15–16.

Terpstra, Vern, and K. David. 1985. *The Cultural Environment of International Business*. Cincinnati, Ohio: South-Western.

Todryk, Lawrence. December 1990. "The Project Manager as Team Builder: Creating an Effective Team." *Project Management Journal*, Vol. 21, No. 4, pp. 17–22.

U.S. Department of Labor, Bureau of Labor-Management Relations and Cooperative Programs. 1984. *Labor-Management Cooperation: Perspectives from the Labor Movement*. Washington, DC.

VanDyk, P. S., P. S. Nel, and P. VanZloedolff. 1992. *Training Management*. Southern Publishers.

Verney, Thomas, Robert Ackelsberg, and Stephen Holoviak. June 1989. "Participation and Worker Productivity." *Quality and Participation Journal*, pp. 74–78.

Verney, Thomas, Stephen Holoviak, and Paula Kirby. August 1986. "Group Development in Quality Circles." *Performance and Instruction Journal*, Vol. 25, No. 6, p. 27.

Walker, S. Lynne. October 9, 1991. "Gen Dyn Execs Reap 2nd Huge Bonus." *San Diego Union*.

Wall Street Journal. December 29, 1992. "An NLRB Ruling."

Welter, Therese R. May 6, 1991. "A Winning Team Begins with You." *Industry Week*, Vol. 240, No. 9, pp. 35, 37–42.

Wickens, Peter. 1987. *The Road to Nissan: Flexibility Quality Teamwork*. London: Macmillan Press.

Williams, Donna, and Stephen Holoviak. September 1990. "Seven Steps to First Impressions." *Training*, Vol. 27, No. 9.

Wright, Peter, and David Taylor. 1984. *Improving Leadership Performance*. Englewood Cliffs, New Jersey: Prentice-Hall.

Yelowitz, Irwin. 1965. *Labor and the Progressive Movement in New York State, 1897–1916*. Ithaca, New York: Cornell University Press.

Zaleznik, Abraham. 1989. *The Managerial Mystique: Restoring Leadership in Business*. New York: Harper and Row, pp. 49, 53, 57.

Index